STUDIES IN ENGL.

WOLFRETON SCHOOL
This book is to be returned on or
before the last date stamped below

WOLFRETON SCHOOL LIBRARY
R08414F0277

Already published in the series:

1. **Milton:** Comus *and* Samson Agonistes by *J. B. Broadbent*
2. **Pope:** The Rape of the Lock by *J. S. Cunningham*
3. **Jane Austen:** Emma by *Frank Bradbrook*
4. **W. B. Yeats:** The Poems by *A. Norman Jeffares*
5. **Chaucer:** The Knight's Tale *and* The Clerk's Tale by *Elizabeth Salter*
6. **Marlowe:** Dr. Faustus by *Philip Brockbank*
7. **Hardy:** The Mayor of Casterbridge by *Douglas Brown*
8. **Webster:** The Duchess of Malfi by *Clifford Leech*
10. **Wordsworth:** The Prelude and other poems by *John F. Danby*
11. **George Eliot:** Middlemarch by *David Daiches*
12. **Conrad:** Lord Jim by *Tony Tanner*
13. **Shakespeare:** Hamlet by *Kenneth Muir*
14. **Shakespeare:** Macbeth by *John Russell Brown*
15. **Shakespeare:** King Lear by *Nicholas Brooke*
16. **Shakespeare:** Much Ado About Nothing by *J. R. Mulryne*
17. **Donne:** Songs and Sonets by *A. J. Smith*
18. **Marvell:** Poems by *Dennis Davison*
19. **Dickens:** Great Expectations by *R. George Thomas*
20. **Emily Brontë:** Wuthering Heights by *Frank Goodridge*
21. **Shakespeare:** The Merchant of Venice by *A. D. Moody*
22. **Tennyson:** In Memoriam by *K. W. Gransden*
23. **Fielding:** Tom Jones by *I. Ehrenpreis*
24. **Shakespeare:** Henry IV by *R. J. Beck*
25. **Shakespeare:** As You Like It by *Michael Jamieson*
26. **Shakespeare:** The Winter's Tale by *A. D. Nuttall*
28. **D. H. Lawrence:** Sons and Lovers by *Gāmini Salgādo*
29. **Dickens:** Little Dorrit by *J. C. Reid*
30. **E. M. Forster:** A Passage to India by *John Colmer*
31. **Shakespeare:** Richard II by *A. R. Humphreys*
32. **Henry James:** The Portrait of a Lady by *David Galloway*
33. **Gissing:** New Grub Street by *P. J. Keating*
34. **Blake:** The Lyric Poetry by *John Holloway*
35. **Shakespeare:** A Midsummer Night's Dream by *Stephen Fender*
36. **Mark Twain:** Huckleberry Finn by *Jonathan Raban*
37. **T. S. Eliot:** The Waste Land by *Helen Williams (2nd edition)*
38. **Swift:** Gulliver's Travels by *Angus Ross*
39. **Shakespeare:** The Tempest by *John Russell Brown*
40. **Conrad:** Nostromo by *Juliet McLauchlan*
41. **Tennyson:** The Early Poems by *John Pettigrew*
42. **Golding:** Lord of the Flies by *John S. Whitley*
43. **Hardy:** Tess of the D'Urbervilles by *Bruce Hugman*
44. **Shakespeare:** Antony and Cleopatra by *Robin Lee*
45. **Webster:** The White Devil by *D. C. Gunby*
46. **D. H. Lawrence:** The Rainbow by *Frank Glover-Smith*
47. **Shakespeare:** Othello by *Juliet McLauchlan*
48. **Virginia Woolf:** To the Lighthouse by *Stella McNichol*
49. **Pope:** The Dunciad by *Howard Erskine-Hill*
50. **James Joyce:** Ulysses by *Michael Mason*
51. **Tobias Smollett:** The Expedition of Humphry Clinker by *John Valdimir Price*
52. **James Joyce:** A Portrait of the Artist as a Young Man by *Harvey Peter Sucksmith*
53. **Gerard Manley Hopkins:** The Poems by *R. K. R. Thornton*
54. **Charles Dickens:** Bleak House by *Grahame Smith*
55. **Samuel Richardson:** Clarissa by *Anthony Kearney*
56. **Wordsworth and Coleridge:** The Lyrical Ballads by *Stephen Prickett*
57. **Shakespeare:** Measure for Measure by *Nigel Alexander*
58. **Shakespeare:** Coriolanus by *Brian Vickers*
59. **Chaucer:** Troilus and Criseyde by *A. C. Spearing*

GOLDING:
LORD OF THE FLIES

by

JOHN S. WHITLEY

*Lecturer in English and American Literature,
University of Sussex*

EDWARD ARNOLD

© JOHN S. WHITLEY, 1970

First published 1970 by
Edward Arnold (Publishers) Ltd.,
25 Hill Street, London, W1X 8LL

Reprinted 1969, 1974, 1976

Cloth edition ISBN: 0 7131 5503 5
Paper edition ISBN: 0 7131 5504 3

All Rights Reserved. No part of this publication may be reproduced, stored in a retrieval system, or transmitted in any form or by any means, electronic, mechanical, photocopying, recording or otherwise, without the prior permission of Edward Arnold (Publishers) Ltd.

For my parents

Printed in Great Britain by
The Camelot Press Ltd, Southampton

General Preface

The object of this series is to provide studies of individual novels, plays and groups of poems and essays which are known to be widely read by students. The emphasis is on clarification and evaluation; biographical and historical facts, while they may be discussed when they throw light on particular elements in a writer's work, are generally subordinated to critical discussion. What kind of work is this? What exactly goes on here? How good is this work, and why? These are the questions that each writer will try to answer.

It should be emphasized that these studies are written on the assumption that the reader has already read carefully the work discussed. The objective is not to enable students to deliver opinions about works they have not read, nor is it to provide ready-made ideas to be applied to works that have been read. In one sense all critical interpretation can be regarded as foisting opinions on readers, but to accept this is to deny the advantages of any sort of critical discussion directed at students or indeed at anybody else. The aim of these studies is to provide what Coleridge called in another context 'aids to reflection' about the works discussed. The interpretations are offered as suggestive rather than as definitive, in the hope of stimulating the reader into developing further his own insights. This is after all the function of all critical discourse among sensible people.

Because of the interest which this kind of study has aroused, it has been decided to extend it first from merely English literature to include also some selected works of American literature and now further to include selected works in English by Commonwealth writers. The criterion will remain that the book studied is important in itself and is widely read by students.

DAVID DAICHES

Contents

1.	INTRODUCTION	7
2.	THE TEXT	25
	Introductions and Foreshadowings	25
	The Limitations of the Fable	39
	Beasts and Violence	41
	The Sense of an Ending	51
3.	SELECT BIBLIOGRAPHY	57
	NOTES	60
	INDEX	63

Note. The Bibliography gives the original date of publication of each work. The dates given in the footnotes are those of the editions consulted and need not be those of the original editions.

Acknowledgments

The author and publishers of this study wish to thank Faber and Faber Ltd. for their permission to use extracts from *Lord of the Flies*, and Richard Hughes and Chatto and Windus Ltd. for extracts from *A High Wind in Jamaica*.

1. Introduction

Nature, with an equal mind,
Sees all her sons at play . . .
                        Matthew Arnold

William Golding's first novel, *Lord of the Flies* (1954), one of the most widely-read, widely-admired novels in the English language in the last quarter of a century, has been called a fable. John Peter, in a pioneering article on Golding's work,[1] has this to say in explanation of the term:

> Fables are those narratives which leave the impression that their purpose was anterior, some initial thesis or contention which they are apparently concerned to embody and express in concrete terms. Fables always give the impression that they were preceded by the conclusion which it is their function to draw, though of course it is doubtful whether any author foresees his conclusions as fully as this, and unlikely that his work would be improved if he did.[2]

Golding himself, in his essay, 'Fable', has used the term to describe *Lord of the Flies*, suggesting that

> The fabulist is a moralist. He cannot make a story without a human lesson tucked away in it.[3]

These comments suggest that the initial idea or thesis which governs the book can be briefly summarised. *Lord of the Flies* is governed by the idea that man is a fallen creature. Reacting against the Romantic notion that man is basically noble if freed from the fetters of society, Golding insists that evil is inherent in man; a terrifying force which he must recognise and control. 'The fabulist is didactic', remarks Golding, and 'desires to inculcate a moral lesson'.[4] We could say that Swift wrote *Gulliver's Travels* from the initial idea that man is a lost creature unless he uses his supreme gift of reason, and that all four voyages reflect this lack of or studied indifference to the right use of reason either in the creatures whom Gulliver meets, or in Gulliver himself.

Fictional works which could be included within these definitions, such as *Pilgrim's Progress*, *Gulliver's Travels*, *Candide*, *Animal Farm*, and *Lord of the Flies*, have one aspect in common, the avoidance of contemporary social reality. Gulliver is taken on journeys to fantastic lands;

Animal Farm shows us the political chicaneries of the farmyard and *Lord of the Flies* allows us to join young castaways on a tropical island. All these works, of course, finally have much to say about man and society, but the necessity of maintaining a clear thesis requires their authors first to remove the action of the novel from the complexities of society in order to say what they have to say about it. *Robinson Crusoe* (1719) is supremely a novel of its time. It takes man out of the encumbrances of society, on to a desert island, to prove a strong social point; that man is capable, through education, of progress: that man, in a laissez-faire society, is capable of an infinite expansion of potential. It is a book about how man can use his brains and hands to manipulate the objects around him: not merely to survive but positively to triumph. When Defoe returns to a social setting, in *Moll Flanders* (1722), the expansion of Moll's potential cannot remain a social point capable of neat summary because Moll has to deal with other people, thus giving rise to multiple (if inconsistent) ironic reflections upon her capitalist enterprise.

The fable fosters the idea of pattern. If you begin with an initial thesis, then you must take care that no irrelevant material is introduced; no characters who do not fit into the idea or illustrate some aspect of the idea; no action which exists independent of the symbolic action at the core of the book. Perhaps the pattern of the book, the brilliant way in which Golding, through a remarkably tight structure, plays the initial theme over and over, accounts for some of its popularity. The fact that everything unfolds clearly before the reader—the island, the predicament of the boys, the distinctions in character which are to prove fatal, the futile attempts at order and democracy, the pull away towards savagery and primitive ritual, the unbearable tension mounting to a climax—means that we follow this world in embryo, this break-up of values, from start to finish (in a short novel) with nothing to sidetrack us. In most non-fables (social novels) this cannot happen. In a novel by George Eliot or Henry James there is no thesis to be fleshed out but a complicated situation of human motive and interaction where the novelist is at pains to record every ambiguity in dialogue and every shift in emotional response. In the non-fable, the writer is concerned to present a life surprisingly close to our own, a mass of complexities of character and situation; a maze through which the individual (and the reader) must try and find his way. All novelists must create some sort of pattern in order to form a whole, a unified artistic experience, but in many modern non-fables the pattern must somehow be made to reflect a lack of pattern. This is often done by balancing the reader's response against that of a central character who tries to impose a plan upon experience. Thus Henry Fleming, in Stephen Crane's *The Red Badge of Courage* (1895), tries to view war as a struggle for Homeric glory, and nature as a force deeply involved and interested in man's life, whereas the 'pattern' of the novel shows *us* war as a chaotic series of unconnected impressions. Augie March, in Saul Bellow's *The Adventures of Augie March* (1953), persistently clings to his hope of understanding his quest in life, only to end in laughter at the enigma of experience; whereas the reader, at the end, has a greater recognition of Augie's direction than he has himself.

Yet if the preceeding comments represent a rough general distinction between the fable and non-fable, their applicability to *Lord of the Flies* creates dangers which need to be recognised. The term 'fable' has close links with 'allegory', certainly in its earlier stages. It is difficult to call Aesop's fable of the tortoise and the hare an allegory because although the moral of the fable:

> A naturally gifted man, through lack of application, is often beaten by a plodder[5]

suggests that the tortoise = the plodder, while the hare = the naturally gifted man, this equation can only be arrived at once we have consulted the tagged-on moral, not during our reading of the fable. In an allegory the abstract meaning moves along in parallel to the surface story by way of one-to-one relationships. Meanings are worked out in terms of A = B, C = D, as in Book One of *The Faerie Queene* where, on the simplest level, Una = unity hence truth, while Duessa = duality hence falsehood. When we read *The Pilgrim's Progress* we are obviously aware that we must move quickly from the characters on to a higher plane where we are considering the values embodied in those characters. In the cases of *The Pilgrim's Progress* or *Everyman* both 'fable' and 'allegory' could be applied because the wish to create a fable, hence to move away from contemporary social reality, is clearly aided by creating an allegorical, 'unreal' landscape and characters who are no more than allegorical types, i.e., Fellowship, Knowledge, Beauty.

With the rise of the novel, however, comes an increasing sophistication and a playing down of allegorical possibilities. Defoe, despite removing Robinson Crusoe from everyday social reality, is concerned to create verisimilitude, to make us believe in Crusoe as a man and the island as a real island. Once you begin to do this, allegory becomes impossible. We can define a general truth for Defoe's novel, but this truth is worked out through the reality of objects and incidents, never by making those objects and incidents precisely correspond to aspects of a higher reality.

Golding is also concerned to flesh out his truth as accurately as possible and few could deny the successful reality which he gives to the boys and their environment. The island is described with a consistently loving detail:

> The edge of the lagoon became a streak of phosphorescence which advanced minutely, as the great wave of the tide flowed. The clear water mirrored the clear sky and the angular bright constellations. The line of phosphorescence bulged about the sand grains and little pebbles; it held them each in a dimple of tension, then suddenly accepted them with an inaudible syllable and moved on.[6]

If the island must be made as realistic as possible, so must its inhabitants, if Golding is to cover the bones of his thesis and force us to accept it as saying something relevant about human beings. Realism is given to the actions of the boys, as when Maurice tries to calm the 'littluns' who begin to cry at a council meeting:

> Maurice saved them. He cried out.
> 'Look at me!'
> He pretended to fall over. He rubbed his rump and sat on the twister so that he fell in the grass. He clowned badly; but Percival and the others noticed and sniffed and laughed. Presently they were all laughing so absurdly that the biguns joined in.[7]

The speech, too, is realistic, as when Samneric, having fallen asleep, awakes just in time to save the fire from dying:

> 'That was near.'
> 'He'd have been—'
> 'Waxy.'
> 'Huh.'
> For a few moments the twins watched the fire in silence. Then Eric sniggered.
> 'Wasn't he waxy?'
> 'About the—'
> 'Fire and the pig.'
> 'Lucky he went for Jack, 'stead of us.'

'Huh. Remember old Waxy at school?'
'"Boy—you-are-driving-me-slowly-insane!"'[8]

Much critical comment has been given to Golding's use of symbolism. Unlike allegorical figures, the full impact of symbols can only be measured when we reach the end of the book. They build up in a pyramid form to merge with the total design of the book and they take their power not simply from their relationship to our own experience and consciousness, but also from their place in the book, their possible relationships to other symbols around them and to the symbolic structure as a whole. If verisimilitude reduces the possibilities of allegory, extensive symbolism virtually banishes them, because symbols, working by a process of agglomeration, gathering around themselves denser and denser layers of meaning, swiftly break up any simple two-layer pattern. The point is made clearer if we ask ourselves such questions as: what does Piggy represent? What does the fire represent? If Piggy is A, what is the B that he should equal? If Piggy equals common sense, then does his death simply mean the death of common sense on the island? If the fire equals some sort of adherence to civilised values, why does it kill the littlun with the mulberry-coloured birthmark? Why does it become an agent of devastation? It will be the task of this essay to provide some tentative answers to these questions, but only by swiftly breaking any arbitrary allegorical pattern. Golding develops his central thesis in a mixture of symbolism and realism which provides psychological accuracy and depth of human motive and interaction unprecedented in previous works known under the term 'fable'.

Four of William Golding's novels make use of isolated surroundings. *Lord of the Flies* (1954) takes place on a coral island; *The Inheritors* (1955) in prehistory; *Pincher Martin* (1956) on a rock in the Atlantic and *The Spire* (1964) in the building and environs of a medieval cathedral. In his first novel Golding seems deliberately to have created a setting which strongly taps the reader's memory of literary history, and as it seems clear that we are expected to bring to our reading a literary background against which the present action can be played, often ironically, it will be well to sketch in some of that background.

The island environment naturally forms part of the romantic dream of the post-Industrial Revolution man: the liberal view of man as essentially noble and being able to re-create that nobility in what Professor R. W. B. Lewis has called an *apeiron*,[9] an area of possibility which is unpopulated and far from the ceaseless travail and automatic gestures of a mechanised society. This feeling acquires its strongest impetus in the Romantic writers. Rousseau, attempting to cut man adrift from the twin fetters of Church and State, demanded that man derive much of his education from a willingness to return to and understand nature, to allow nature to form a boy's character by suspending rational, analytical judgments and permitting full scope to an intuitive perception of the unity of man and nature. Rousseau, however, never envisaged a state of permanent withdrawal from society. Perceptions of one's own heart, which came from an immersion in nature, could be taken back as a benefit to society once the 'sleep of reason' had ended. But in the lesser Romantic writers, in particular Chateaubriand and James Fenimore Cooper, there is less of a concern with what happens to man when he can no longer maintain himself in the isolated environment. Chateaubriand, although he knew relatively little about North American Indians, writes about them extensively in 'Atala', 'René' and 'Les Natchez'. He sees Indians as the last examples of noble, harmonious men because they are at one with their wild, uncultivated surroundings. Removed from civilised society, they can teach civilised man about that integrity of body and spirit which he has lost. A similar attitude exists in Cooper's Leatherstocking novels where white man and red man found a viable relationship between themselves and with a wilderness they thoroughly understand. It is a 'dream among the trees' threatened only by the representatives of a corrupt society, the red-haired temptress or the lying soldier.

After the Romantic period, members of the industrial society are quick to realise the transience and impossibility of the dream. The country/city dichotomy is prominent and simplistic in such early Dickens novels as *The Old Curiosity Shop* and *Nicholas Nickleby* but by the time of *Great Expectations* it has vanished. If the countryside of the later novel has Joe Gargery it also has Orlick. Defying nineteenth-century industrial society as he frequently did, Carlyle sometimes dreams of a hut in the wilderness, but then realises that he has to reject it. Even as recent a novelist of the industrial society as Alan Sillitoe (and Sillitoe's 'findings' are often close to those of sociologists: compare *Saturday Night and Sunday Morning* with John Goldthorpe's study of the Vauxhall assembly-line workers) makes his central characters, especially Arthur Seaton in *Saturday Night and Sunday Morning* and Brian Seaton in *Key To The Door*, long for a hut in the forest, an escape from the mindless round of factory life. Yet this is only a dream-escape. The nearest Arthur can come to it is to fish in the canal; and the fishing in the canal is, in the end, made representative of Arthur's residue of strength, whereby he can enter a new relationship in marriage with Doreen, and can do it with a certain amount of hope. By a neatly ironic reversal Brian Seaton dreams of a hut in the wilderness and gets it, a radio operations hut in the middle of the rice fields of Malaya during the monsoon season. The rain comes in through the roof and he is extremely miserable and lonely. These ironic tatters are often all that remains in contemporary literature of the liberal dream.

Yet sometimes it re-emerges strongly, as in an American novel published three years before *Lord of the Flies* and a book which Golding may well have been remembering as he wrote, J. D. Salinger's *The Catcher in The Rye*. Deliberately imitating the form of *Huckleberry Finn*, Salinger takes an American adolescent, Holden Caulfield who, despite his flip talk, is the kind of innocent who rubs dirty words off walls so that little girls will not have to see them, and takes him on a journey from outside the city, at Pencey School, into New York, a nightmarish place full of pimps and whores and perverts. One of the chief perverts turns out to be the man, his former schoolteacher, to whom he turns in his desperate need for affection. Finally he can only place his idea of beauty in his vision of the small girl skating in Central Park and in his relationship with his lovely but very young sister, Phoebe. He can find no viable relationship with adult society. As in *Huckleberry Finn*, though less objectively, we are presented with the consciousness of an adolescent who does not know how much truth he is telling. It is a view of society seen through the eyes of an innocent and receiving support from the author. That is to say, if we have to place blame for man's inhumanity to man, then this traditionally liberal novel insists that we place it on society and the institutions it has created to overlook man. We must not place it in man's heart, for that is still full of love and joy if only society would grant him an outlet for it.

Previous comments on *Robinson Crusoe* have suggested, however, that writers may use the isolated environment to uphold current social philosophies rather than counteract them. Defoe's novel is a hymn to individualism, an echo of the great confidence which the early eighteenth century placed in 'economic man'. In order to maintain this confidence Defoe frees Crusoe from any complicating encumbrances. There are no women. He refuses to countenance the possibilities of regression to primitivism, though the novel does demonstrate (possibly unconsciously) the dangers of that egocentricity which runs concurrent to the triumph of individualism, for in the only human relationship treated at any length in the book, that between Robinson and Friday, it is quite clear that Friday is regarded as a thing to be used, like a spade or rifle. It is a book which celebrates manual labour. Nature allows Crusoe to give vent to a pietistic streak. Nature will reveal to him the glory of God but it is also there to be exploited, made to produce sustenance through the labour of man's hands. This ensures a usefully combined worship of God and man. These features are reproduced a century and a half later in another novel which uses shipwreck on an island as a means of reinforcing the current beliefs of society, R. M. Ballantyne's *The Coral Island* (1857).

That *The Coral Island* was in Golding's mind when he wrote *Lord of the Flies* is quite clear. There are two references to the earlier work and one or two definite links between the books. For example, quite early in Ballantyne's novel, Ralph discusses the expeditions that he, Jack and Peterkin made (the similarity in names is the most obvious link between the two books):

> ... when we travelled along the sands which extended almost in an unbroken line of glistening white around the island, we marched abreast, as we found this method more sociable and in every way more pleasant. Jack, being the tallest, walked next the sea, and Peterkin marched between us, as by this arrangement, either of us could talk to him or he to us, while if Jack and I happened to wish to converse together, we could conveniently do so over Peterkin's head.[10]

Compare this with the first exploration of the island in Golding's novel:

> Ralph, Jack and Simon jumped off the platform and walked along the sand past the bathing pool. Piggy hung bumbling behind them.
> 'If Simon walks in the middle of us,' said Ralph, 'then we could talk over his head.'
> The three of them fell into step. This meant that every now and then Simon had to do a double shuffle to catch up with the others.[11]

There is also at least one carefully-created link in the use made of details of the islands. At one point, needing light, Ballantyne's boys use candle nuts. In keeping with the very different spirit of the later novel, Golding's boys decide that the nuts cannot be lit.

It is clear, then, that Ballantyne's novel is very much present to Golding and one way to look at *Lord of the Flies* is that it is a twentieth-century inversion of a nineteenth-century thesis, for, just as *Robinson Crusoe* backs up the early eighteenth-century idea of individualism, so *The Coral Island* reinforces the Victorian ideal of progress. As an early example of nineteenth-century imperialism it does suggest, unlike *Lord of the Flies*, that the British are best at everything. It is a book that rides the buoyant wave of Victorian optimism and stiffens confidence in the idea of progress. In both books the island is beautiful and the initial reactions to the 'dream' place are similar:

> 'My dear boys, we're set up for life! It must be the ancient Paradise —hurrah!'[12]

> Here at last was the imagined but never fully realised place leaping into real life. Ralph's lips parted in a delighted smile and Piggy, taking this smile to himself as a mark of recognition, laughed with pleasure.[13]

but the actions and reactions of Ballantyne's boys are usually diametrically opposed to their modern counterparts. An American student of mine once remarked that Golding's boys were British and therefore incompetent, but the reverse is true of the characters in *The Coral Island*. Taking several leaves out of Robinson Crusoe's book, they do very well for themselves, making a boat, a shelter, various utensils and stuffing themselves in astonishing fashion:

> There was, first of all, the little pig, then there were the taro root and the yam and the potato and six plums, and lastly the wood pigeon. Altogether this was decidedly the most luxurious supper we had enjoyed for many a day.[14]

Golding's boys, who are younger, are deliberately made incompetent since this facilitates their retreat into primitive ritual. They lack the ballast of the Victorian work ethic.

The evil of Ballantyne's novel is wholly externalised, largely in the cannibals who live on surrounding islands. The Romantic view would show Leatherstocking and Chingachgook threatened in their wilderness paradise by the forces of civilisation, but here it is precisely the boys' triumphant attempts to maintain the values of Victorian civilisation that ensure their triumph over the atavism recorded in the cannibals. The location of evil outside the characters allows for the recourse to piety already noted in *Robinson Crusoe*:

> They told me of thousands of beautiful, fertile islands that had been formed by a small creature called the coral insect, where summer reigned nearly all the year around, where the trees were laden with

almost constant harvest of luxurious fruit, where the climate was almost perpetually delightful, yet where, strange to say, men were wild, bloodthirsty savages, excepting in those favoured isles to which the Gospel of our Saviour had been conveyed.[15]

At times Ballantyne seems to teeter on the brink of a 'modern' subtlety. There are horrific descriptions of atrocities, and Ralph, upon witnessing a tribal war, remarks:

> I felt my heart grow sickened at the sight of this bloody battle, and would fain have turned away, but a species of fascination seemed to hold me down and glue my eyes upon the combatants.[16]

Such a remark (and there are several) could be taken to suggest a tendency towards atavism lurking *within* the characters, but, as in many minor Victorian novels, this remains an element which the writer either has not recognised or cannot bring himself to countenance. Hence this fascination seems only accidental and the boys conquer the external evil because, in the happy, idyllic state of the island, their relationship never alters. They triumph through togetherness:

> There was indeed no note of discord whatever in the symphony we played together on that sweet coral island. And I am now persuaded that this was owing to our having been all tuned to the same key, namely that of love. Yes, we loved one another with such fervency while we lived on that island, and for the matter of that we love each other still . . .[17]

a togetherness which maintains the Victorian ethic of the family, a civilised community writ small.

In terms of these two opposing areas of possibility, the escape from civilisation or the triumph of civilisation, Golding's boys have the worst of both worlds. When they first land on the island they strike the reader as very much boys from a civilised society, but they do not seem to have learnt from civilisation. They cannot exploit nature, only wreck it. On the other hand, nature cannot 'teach' them anything, in the Rousseauistic or Wordsworthian traditions. Ralph, as leader, elects to go off and discover what the beast really is, and on his way he looks down from the narrow neck on to the expanse of the sea:

> Now he saw the landsman's view of the swell, and it seemed like the breathing of some stupendous creature. Slowly the water sank upon the rocks, revealing pink tables of granite, strange growths of coral,

polyp, and weed. Down, down the waters went, whispering like the winds among the heads of the forest.[18]

There is an intense awareness throughout the novel of man's physical surroundings. The island and sea are described beautifully, but often by Golding rather than the boys, because it is clear that nature (its beauty may be usefully contrasted with the increasing savagery on the island) has no connection with the human actions. The physical surroundings do nothing to advance or detract from man's awareness of his predicament. When one of the characters observes his surroundings his view is always coloured by his mood. In the previous quotation Ralph is desperately frightened, half despising the idea of the existence of a beastie, and half terrified at the prospect of meeting one. Naturally, in this frame of mind, the sea becomes mysterious and menacing. Yet Golding is also making his own attitude clear. Man is alone in his quest for the knowledge of evil, and his isolation is enforced by the relentless ebb and flow of the sea. The departure to sea of Simon's body is related with a lingering sense of wonder, but no problems are solved. It represents a cessation of suffering, a cleansing, but neither a revitalisation nor a significant change. The natural surround is as it was before, so is the human situation. In this respect, Golding is heir to such naturalists as Stephen Crane:

> A man said to the universe:
>
> 'Sir, I exist!'
>
> 'However,' replied the universe,
> 'The fact has not created in me
> A sense of obligation.'[19]

The child's dream of freedom from the restrictions of adult society mirrors the civilised adult's dream of freedom from the burdens of civilised society. In both cases the dream becomes nightmare. There is no idyll. Individualism leads to regression and brotherhood is impossible. The boys in *Lord of the Flies* begin with a kind of comradeship roughly comparable to that in *The Coral Island*:

> Jack and Ralph smiled at each other with shy liking. . . .[20]

but it quickly breaks down and its destruction is one of the most poignant truths of the book. This pessimistic view of man has been labelled 'Calvinistic' in suitable opposition to 'liberal', but it matters little whether we say, in religious terms, that the novel shows the reality of original sin or, in post-Freudian terms, that it shows the inevitable triumph of the Id when man is taken out of the security of his social position. What is shown is that man, in such an isolated situation, can control neither his environment nor his inner desires. Yet neither does the novel uphold the values of civilised society. If the free individual in nature brings death upon himself, civilisation can send only tokens of death, like the dead airman or the heavily-armed cruiser.

If the preceding remarks keep suggesting that the boys are representatives of 'man' it is as well to remember that they only achieve this status by being presented as very real boys. Just as Golding overturns various island myths, so he again asks us to bring to our reading of *Lord of the Flies* some understanding of past views of children in order to see the different use he makes of them here.

It is significant that an interest in children in literature grew up with the Romantic movement, especially in the writings of Rousseau and Wordsworth, for it is very like their interest in nature and the past. To them the child represents a pre-Industrial Revolution innocence, an integrity of being based on an unlimited capacity for wonder and fancy. In the dehumanising industrial world man's only hope of survival lies in allowing free rein to this capacity for wonder, particularly away from the towns. The eighteenth century tended, in its writings, to treat the child as a small adult. This is not Rousseau's idea at all. He is interested in the 'sleep of reason' allowing children to be children in order that they can become 'whole' adults. Blake, in his 'Songs of Innocence', relates the activities of children, in their spontaneity, to the activities of nature, but the 'Songs of Experience' show an urban world where these harmonious links are destroyed. For Wordsworth the child might have intuitive perceptions of eternal truth which adults, hemmed in by urban society, by the 'shades of the prison house', can rarely even glimpse. As urban society expands, the Victorian novelists come to see the child more and more as a victim of social pressures, of a society obsessed with the idea of progress. Against this, as nature loses its force, Romantic viewpoints become platitudes. Oliver Twist is brought to health in a typically idealised rural surround; Charles Kingsley's Alton Locke, amid the slums, dreams of Pacific Islands, of the delights of nature which he places against the severities of his puritanical mother. Whereas the Romantics often discuss the child as part of a human development, nineteenth-century novelists come to see childhood as a means of escape, and that all is lost when adulthood arrives. The Victorians, as Peter Coveney[21] observes, seemed to have a dual view of the child as holy innocent and miserable sinner: miserable sinner in proportion to the way he fails to live up to that picture of him as a holy innocent. Thus a good deal of sentimentality and morbidity becomes involved in their literary treatment of children. In his earlier novels Charles Dickens makes the death of a child symptomatic of the horrors of society; in *The Mill on the Floss* George Eliot describes Maggie Tulliver's childhood in joyously evocative detail but loses objectivity in the second half and presents society as a prison-house which crushes Maggie; in the later nineteenth-century novelists, like Marie Correlli and J. M. Barrie, all that remains is regret at the passing of childhood and relief at the death of a child because the burden of adulthood is thus avoided.

The myth of the child as innocent was brutally overturned with the publication, in 1905, of Freud's *Three Contributions to a Theory of Sex*, which included a discussion of 'infantile sexuality'. Freud discovered that the sexual disturbances of many of his patients could be traced to incidents in very early childhood and, from this, elaborated a theory of stages of eroticism through which a child passes on his way to 'genital primacy' at the age of five. This theory, discussing among other things the Oedipus complex (the early incest-wish among children) is completely at odds with the Victorian myth which saw sexual passion as the devil's work, corrupting innocence. Two pre-Freudian novels by Henry James, *What Maisie Knew* (1897) and *The Turn of the Screw* (1898) would seem to suggest the possibility of sexual awareness in children, but both turn out to avoid the issue. Maisie is a beautiful child surrounded by adult depravity but she remains innocent despite all she sees; and the two children in *The Turn of the Screw* are never three-dimensional because James sees them as receptacles either for the genuine corruptive influence of Quint and Miss Jessel or for the sexually-obsessed fantasies of the governess. As we don't know which they must remain shadowy.[22]

Not until twenty-five years after Freud had published his theories did a novelist create a vehicle for them. Richard Hughes's *A High Wind in Jamaica* (1929) has had a remarkable influence in persuading twentieth-century readers that children can be cruel and have no sense of responsibility to anyone. Hughes tries to see his children objectively, to insist that the child's world is amoral, quite separate from that of adults and unavailable to discussion in terms of adult values. Two deaths occur in a hurricane, that of Sam, the negro servant, and that of a pet cat, Tabby, and Hughes makes it quite clear which is more important to the children:

> The death of Tabby, at times, seemed a horror beyond all bearing. It was her first intimate contact with death and a death of violence, too. The death of Old Sam had no such effect—there is, after all, a vast difference between the death of a negro and the death of a favourite cat.[23]

Later, when the eldest child, John, has fallen out of a barn-loft and broken his neck, the children's reaction to it is not at all what the reader expects:

> Yet, as if by some mute flash of understanding, no-one commented on his absence; no-one questioned Margaret and she offered no information. Neither then nor thereafter was his name ever mentioned by anybody, and if you had known the children intimately, you would never have known from them that he had ever existed.[24]

In his desire to create an entirely separate world for the children, Hughes sometimes verges on the bizarre:

> Being nearly four years old she (Laura) was certainly a child, and children are human if one allows the term human a wide sense. But she had not altogether ceased to be a baby and babies, of course, are not human, they are animals, and have a very ancient and ramified culture as cats have and fishes and even snakes, but much more complicated and vivid, since babies are, after all, one of the most developed species of the lower vertebrates.
>
> Possibly a case may be made out that children are not human, either, but I should not accept it. Agreed that their minds are not just more ignorant and stupider than ours, but differ in kind of thinking, are mad, in fact, but one can, by an effort of will and imagination, think like a child, at least in a partial degree ... while one can no more think like a baby ... than one can think like a bee.[25]

The differences between the two worlds are made clear in the relationship between the children and the pirates. When Emily stabs the Dutch captain to death in her fear, a death the pirates wrongly accredit to Margaret, they throw Margaret overboard because they feel that this action, along with her promiscuity, has belied the child they think she ought to be. The novel is set in the nineteenth century and the pirates have a fuddled Victorian notion of the child. When they come face-to-face with actions by the children which block this view they are appalled and the children are shunned:

They were treated with a detached severity not wholly divorced from fear, as if these unfortunate men at last realised what diabolic yeast had been introduced into their lump.[26]

At the very end of the novel the pirates are sent to the gallows for the murder which Emily committed. The negro cook sums up his feelings about this:

> 'You know that I die innocent. Anything I have done I was forced to do by the rest of you, but I am not sorry. I would rather die now innocent than in a few years guilty of some great sin.'[27]

Here we have an adult talking as though he were an innocent child bound to do sin in future, whereas the sin for which he is being punished has been committed by the child, and the pirates have in fact been innocent. They have been destroyed because they saw the children as angelic, whereas the reader's position at the end of the novel is analogous to that of Mr. Bas-Thornton as he looks at his daughter, Emily, lying asleep:

> But as he stood now watching her his sensitive eyes communicated to him an emotion that was not pity and was not delight. He realised, with a sudden painful shock, that he was afraid of her. But surely it was some trick of the candlelight or of her indisposition, that gave her face momentarily that inhuman, stony, basilisk look.[28]

Hughes is not claiming that the children are 'original sinners'. He posits them as a race of beings alien to adult morality. No wonder that 'basilisk' seems a curiously appropriate epithet.

Golding follows Hughes in emphasising the almost gratuitous cruelty of the boys; their sexuality (E. L. Epstein has compared the killing of the sow to an 'Oedipal wedding night')[29] and their 'irrational' behaviour. Yet Golding, as a fabulist, has to do more. He has to ensure that connections are steadily made between the boys' world and the adult society of which they are a microcosm. The children of Hughes's book, although an isolated unit when viewed by the adults, are not a unit at all because they have no sense of responsibility to each other. The boys in *Lord of the Flies* are forced into a community which reflects the disorder and terror of the larger world just as the island community of *The Coral Island* reflected the smug security of its macrocosm. Thus Golding has to present us with post-Freudian realism of boys as we can see and hear them every time we pass a school playing-field at the same time as he must maintain their symbolic presence in the pattern of the novel if the larger truths of the fable are to be ascertained. Two examples should help to show how successfully he accomplishes this.

The character of Piggy is firmly grounded in reality by his nickname, one common in English schools and one which immediately conjures up a physical appearance: fat, clumsy, generally good-natured and not very good at games. From this naturally follows the extension into excessive rationality, yoked with such physical discomforts as myopia, asthma, diarrhoea and sweat. It is right that he should have a lower-class tone and ungrammatical diction, should rest with the civilised values of Auntie and the sweet shop, and should be at once the voice of reason among the yahoos and a fat, unpleasant little boy. In other words, at every turn Piggy fulfils one of the requirements of realism in a novel, when the reader acknowledges: 'Yes, such a person could only act in such a way given these circumstances.' Yet Piggy is just as firmly grounded in the symbolism of the book. It is ironic that the pig is first the beast, then the food left for the beast, and then the lord of the flies, at the same time as the name is given to the most rational being on the island. The irony attached to the name becomes even more intricate as the novel progresses. Piggy denies that there could be a beast:

> 'How could there be? What would a beast eat?'

The boys immediately answer with derision:

> 'Pig.'
> 'We eat pig.'
> 'Piggy!'[30]

and it is Piggy whom they ultimately destroy:

> Piggy fell forty feet and landed on his back across that square red rock in the sea. His head opened and stuff came out and turned red. Piggy's arms and legs twitched a bit, like a pig's after it has been killed.[31]

The formal agent of Piggy's death is the terrifying ritual executioner, Roger, and his manner of despatching the unfortunate:

> Roger, with a sense of delirious abandonment, leaned all his weight on the lever[32]

is a deliberate echo of his part in killing the sow:

> Roger found a lodgment for his point and began to push till he was leaning with his whole weight.[33]

The boys do indeed eat the pig and Piggy is destroyed by the pig-eating beast which lurks deep in each one of them.

Golding's knowledge of boys and their lore (he was, for many years, a schoolmaster) is used with great symbolic force and irony in the final chapter of the book. Claire Rosenfield[34] has discussed the progression of the games in the novel; how, at first, they constitute simply a stepping-out of real life into a temporary sphere of activity with no cultural or moral function and then move toward the formation of a primitive society with its own taboos and rituals. As childish fantasy becomes terrifying reality so:

> ... the children move from voluntary play to ritual, from 'only pretending' to reality, from representation to identification.[35]

The irony of this 'progress' is mirrored in the last chapter which is structured along the lines of a children's game of tag. Perhaps twenty children will join the game in a school playground. One child will be 'it' and will try to tag another child. When he does they will link arms, go off in search of a third, and so on. Eventually a stage is arrived at where nineteen of the twenty have been tagged and have linked arms and spread across the playground in order to catch the last survivor. For a time he may elude them, may diddle them as Ralph tries to do:

> If necessary, when the chase came too close, he could charge the cordon while it was still thin, burst through and run back. But run back where? The cordon would turn and sweep again. Sooner or later he would have to sleep or eat, and then he would awaken with hands clawing at him; ... [36]

The object, within the playground, would be for the chain to drive the remaining child into a corner, and this is what the boys attempt to do with Ralph. His corner is the sea. The idea of the game is emphasised by the use of a 'truce term'. Ralph, early in the chapter, thinks about the possibility of discovering that it was only a game, after all; that if he went up to the rock citadel and said 'Pax', everything would be all right and he could go back into the fort. 'Pax' is, according to Iona and Peter Opie, a 'truce term',[37] that part of the game where you can call a temporary halt by touching a previously indicated article, like a dustbin. When touching this object you cannot be tagged and this gives you a breathing space or an opportunity to tie your shoelace. But, at the end of *Lord of the Flies*, the game of tag has become a deadly reality and the hand which gives a friendly tag-pat has been transformed into a stick sharpened at both ends.

To say, with C. B. Cox, that at times 'Golding deliberately makes us forget that these are only young children'[38] or, with Claire Rosenfield, that the boys 'degenerate into adults',[39] is to tell only part of the story. The true power of Golding's novel lies in the consistent presentation of boys on the most realistic level allied to a symbolic structure which increasingly invests their actions with larger meanings involving that capacity for evil inherent in every human heart. Thus we are prepared for the double perspective of the last three pages where we (the readers) can see the boys as savage men while the lieutenant can only see:

> A semicircle of little boys, their bodies streaked with coloured clay, sharp sticks in their hands, . . .[40]

I cannot resist ending this first section with some 'evidence' of the truth of Golding's vision. In 1963 there appeared a film version of *Lord of the Flies*, directed by Peter Brook; a film shot on a small island near Puerto Rico. The conditions of filming thus approximated to the conditions of the novel which some critics have likened to a sociological experiment (i.e., take x number of schoolboys; place them on a deserted island for y length of time and discover what the z of the equation would be). A reporter for an American magazine[41] discovered that, in a much more limited way, a development had occurred in the boy actors similar to that undergone by Golding's protagonists. They acquired some old mimeographing equipment and produced their own magazine, largely composed of stories on the same theme:

> It was a cold, dark night when the monster struck. It was hairy, with long nails and sharp teeth, and stalked through the alleys until it saw a woman. The woman was mangled and torn to bits. There was blood all over the place.[42]

The boys were housed in a disused pineapple cannery where one of them was discovered lobbing one small lizard after another into the whirring blades of a large electric fan. When asked to explain his behaviour he replied that he was curious to see into how many pieces each lizard would be cut up. As the reporter pointed out, one could almost hear Mr. Golding, four thousand miles away, 'chuckling into his beard'.[43]

2. The Text

'*Kyrie Eleison*'

Introductions and foreshadowings

The opening chapter of *Lord of the Flies*[44] puts us in possession of the situation from which the action is to develop. At some time in the future, with much of the world involved in a nuclear war, a plane carrying schoolboys crashes on a tropical island. The plane has apparently split in half, part (containing the pilot and some of the boys) being swept out to sea and part landing in the forest leaving its occupants, all boys aged roughly between seven and twelve, marooned.

The wish-fulfilment nature of the situation, boundless freedom away from the rigours of adult discipline, is soon realised by Ralph:

'Aren't there any grown-ups at all?'
'I don't think so.'
The fair boy said this solemnly; but then the delight of a realised ambition overcame him. In the middle of the scar he stood on his head and grinned at the reversed fat boy.(12)

This particular moment may remind us of adventure novels both for and about children, for example *Tom Sawyer* or any number of books by Enid Blyton, where the plots involve blissful, exciting periods of time away from adult restrictions. But these books are precisely wish-fulfilment because a child never wants total freedom and escape can only be enjoyed with the knowledge that adult society is always there to return to. The major point of separation between *Tom Sawyer* and *Huckleberry Finn* lies in the final comfort offered by adult society to Tom and the mendacity and violence which it constantly displays to Huck. In Golding's novel the original pleasure taken in a world without grown-ups dwindles as most of the boys increasingly become primitive men and Ralph and Piggy, the representatives of rationality, think continually of rescue. When the adult world does appear it is seen in an ironical light and the 'comfort' it offers is severely questioned.

The opening chapter also introduces us with varying degrees of detail, to the most important protagonists and this introduction is made by way of their physical presences, realistic descriptions which uphold Golding's intention to

> '... make them real boys instead of paper cut-outs with no life in them ...'[45]

and yet, this early, prepare us carefully for the symbolic role each will play in the fable. At the outset Ralph accepts the notion of a world without adults and, in his innocence, is pleased with it, but Piggy is always a part of the adult world and can neither understand nor accept the ensuing breakdown in restrictions:

> 'No grown-ups!'
> The fat boy thought for a moment.
> 'That pilot.'(12)

Golding's use of the nickname 'Piggy' has already been discussed and he invests this character with another childish myth, that surrounding spectacles. As the Opies say:

> ... the myth that spectacles denote superior intellect not merely persists, but is taken for granted.[46]

This is thoroughly and seriously worked into the theme of the novel. The fact that Piggy wears spectacles helps toward his rejection because his myopia joins his diarrhoea and his asthma to increase his ugliness, but also quite easily makes the boys, especially Ralph, consider him brainy and we, along with Ralph, will have to examine the extent of his braininess. His physical stature sharply contrasts with Ralph's:

> He [Ralph] was old enough, twelve years and a few months, to have lost the prominent tummy of childhood; and not yet old enough for adolescence to have made him awkward. You could see now that he might make a boxer, as far as width and heaviness of shoulders went, but there was a mildness about his mouth and eyes that proclaimed no devil...(15)

and so do his primary concerns at this point. Ralph insists that his father will rescue them and lolls happily in the water, only to have his reverie broken by the repetition of Piggy's 'common sense' point:

> 'How does he know we're here?'(19)

The progress of the novel will suggest that Piggy's rationality is static, an increasingly desperate adherence to formulae which come to seem absurd as the boys regress to savagery, while Ralph, as Golding has pointed out, is forced to change and grow as he comes to understand 'the fallen nature of man' and to gear his actions to this knowledge.

Ralph and Piggy discover the conch:

> In colour the shell was deep cream, touched here and there with fading pink. Between the point, worn away into a little hole, and the pink lips of the mouth, lay eighteen inches of shell with a slight spiral twist and covered with a delicate, embossed pattern . . .(22)

and use it to call an assembly. It has become one of the most obvious critical points to insist on the symbolic value of the conch, a representation of common-sense and discipline, an object 'accepted in the light of reason and dedicated to social control'.[47] There is much truth in this, but it is necessary to point out that the conch is beautiful because it is part of the island. Its beauty strikes us when the boys find it in the first chapter but then is forgotten as they put it to use. If its destruction at the same time as Piggy's death symbolises the destruction of rationality on the island it also points out the limitations of that rationality. The conch belongs to nature and as soon as man begins to use it, with whatever decent intentions, it is doomed to inadequacy and oblivion. It brings into being assemblies which rapidly disintegrate into horseplay and boredom and even before this happens Golding is anxious to contrast Ralph and Piggy's intentions with indications of the darkness to come, especially in the form of beast images. As the boys come to the first meeting one attracts attention with his shadow:

> Here, the eye was first attracted to a black, bat-like creature that danced on the sand, and only later perceived the body above it. The bat was the child's shadow, shrunk by the vertical sun to a patch between the hurrying feet.(25)

More especially, the choirboys, due to the conformity of their dress, are seen as a creature 'fumbling along' the beach:

> Their bodies, from throat to ankle, were hidden by black cloaks which bore a long silver cross on the left breast and each neck was finished off with a hambone frill.(26)

In Peter Brook's film this produced a marvellous shot which made the marching schoolboys look like part of a thirties' German propaganda film, while the soundtrack played a version of the 'Kyrie Eleison': 'Lord, Have Mercy'. Once a part of the assembly, they:

> ... perched like black birds on the criss-cross trunks and examined Ralph with interest...(28)

rather like vultures waiting for a feast.

After such imagery it seems absolutely right that Jack should elect himself and his choirboys as hunters. Like the Jack of *The Coral Island* he is the principal 'doer' of the novel, the man of action; but a comparison of their two appearances is illuminating:

> Jack Martin was a tall, strapping, broad-shouldered youth of eighteen, with a handsome, good-humoured, firm face. He had had a good education, was clever and hearty and lion-like in his actions, but mild and quiet in disposition.(5-6)

> Inside the floating cloak he was tall, thin, and bony: and his hair was red beneath the black cap. His face was crumpled and freckled, and ugly without silliness. Out of this face stared two light blue eyes, frustrated now, and turning, or ready to turn, to anger.(27)

Jack Martin is a 'flat' character whom Ballantyne packs with all that's best; health, strength, good looks and intelligence: the ideal sixth-former of a typical Victorian public-school story. As a sailor shipwrecked on a deserted island he cannot convince for one moment. We are presented with a cardboard 'type', whereas Golding immediately brings us close to Jack Merridew's physical presence, a presence which both suggests a real boy who may behave in any number of ways and a symbolic character with mythic associations. His red hair automatically suggests a fiery disposition to counter Ralph's lack of 'devil', but on another level red hair has had immemorial associations with the devil. Characters from literature, such as Marlowe's Barabas or Dickens's Fagin, spring readily to mind. Of course, since the theological/moral universes of these two writers differ strongly from Golding's, the identification is easier to make. Fagin *is* evil as against Rose Maylie who *is* good. If there is a 'devil' in *Lord of the Flies*, then he is present in the whole community. Jack merely implies a latent evil in the island situation which is enhanced by his social 'truth', an aristocratic assumption of leadership and a cutting dismissal of underlings. This assumption of leadership, bred by being part of a civilised élite, is maintained when he becomes a member of a primitive élite. The perfect prefect becomes the perfect savage.

The first assembly introduces Simon and, although Golding risks a good deal by giving such a slow build-up to this 'Christ-figure', there are hints about him at this point. His 'faints' point to his condition, an epileptic, and hence to the ways in which he will be treated. Since we are dealing here, as certain anthropologically-based critics have suggested, with a society which stems from a civilised world, is put into an isolated environment and becomes regressive (tracing a backward path to a primitive society with its rituals and taboos), then in a primitive society it has been shown that a person who is unusual, mentally retarded or in some way deviant, is accorded a great deal of respect, as though he or she were in possession of secrets of the universe, rather like Wordsworth's child. In James Fenimore Cooper's *The Deerslayer* (1841), Hetty Hutter, a sweet, pious but mentally-retarded girl, can wander almost at will in a hostile Indian camp because

> ... in many tribes the mentally imbecile and mad were held in a species of religious reverence, receiving from the untutored inhabitants of the forest respect and honour instead of the contumely and neglect it is their fortune to meet with among the more pretending and sophisticated.[48]

Unfortunately, before the society on the island finally regresses to something close to the primitive state, Simon has been killed. There is never a point at which Simon can receive this reverence, instead he is simply regarded as 'batty'. He is isolated from the boys as a result, but Golding uses this isolation, unlike Cooper, to suggest that Simon really is a seer, one whose vision is of quite a different order from that of Piggy or Ralph. Piggy's vision is increasingly shown to be limited because it is too firmly entrenched in the rationale of adult society to be capable of growth and change, while Ralph, the 'man of goodwill and common sense',[49] *does* develop his vision, but only in the most painful, fumbling and limited way. Simon apprehends neither through adherence to social creeds nor attempted rational analysis, but through an intuitive perception of man's nature and the path it must take. By these intuitive flashes he comes at the central truth of the novel:

> '. . . maybe there is a beast . . . maybe it's only us . . .'
> Simon became inarticulate in his effort to express mankind's essential illness. . . . (111)

but it is axiomatic to the theme of the novel that this truth cannot be recognised, and so Simon dies, a death prepared for by his growing isolation and the terrible burden of responsibility he has to bear. Simon's isolation can be compared with that of Roger, who 'kept to himself with an inner intensity of avoidance and secrecy' (29), for Roger is the representative of that black power which must destroy Simon. He is one of those figures who, according to Yeats, 'recede from us into some more powerful life'.[50] Unlike the others his 'boyness' is never stressed and so he becomes a kind of lurker in the shadows, waiting until the situation makes his role plain, who, when he advances upon Samneric 'as one wielding a nameless authority'(224), acquires tremendous symbolic force as a summation of the horror let loose on the island.

Golding concludes the opening chapter with several skilful uses of 'foreshadowing', hints which clearly establish the pattern which the fable must take. These hints create suspense, not as to what will happen, but as to the manner of its happening. Coleridge said that Shakespeare gives us not surprise but expectation and then the satisfaction of completed knowledge. When, in the first scene of *Macbeth*, the three witches chant, 'Fair is foul, and foul is fair', they are not merely pointing to uncertain weather but establishing a see-saw of moral contraries which at once creates suspense and points to Macbeth's wrong choice. Here Golding suggests what will happen in the course of the fable, creating an inevitability reminiscent of Jacobean tragedy. The transiency of the comradeship has already been pointed out and it is reinforced by the voting, the attempted adherence to democratic procedures, a 'toy', and by the description of the first exploration of the island:

> A kind of glamour was spread over them and the scene and they were conscious of the glamour and made happy by it.(33)

The language here suggests that the 'glamour' is no more than a temporary garment, a cloak thrown over the natural surround by the boys at this point, which will be easily stripped away to show the horror beneath. The elements of this initial happy 'adventure' are precisely chosen to await their later, heavily ironic echoes. Here the three boys indulge in a 'mock' fight:

> This time Ralph expressed the intensity of his emotion by pretending to knock Simon down; and soon they were a happy, heaving pile in the under-dusk.(36)

The 'happy' pile is to become first the mob hurling itself upon the terrified sow and then the hysterical savages who, through the intensity of a very different emotion, knock Simon down and never allow him to get up:

... the crowd surged after it, poured down the rock, leapt on to the beast, screamed, struck, bit, tore.(188)

A situation is given early in the novel, coloured by one sort of mood, and then repeated later, coloured by an opposing mood, to underline the physical and emotional changes and create tension through the ironies involved. Early in *The Coral Island*, as Jack, Ralph and Peterkin are exploring, they hear a rumbling:

> In another moment an enormous rock came crashing through the shrubbery, followed by a cloud of dust and small stones, and flew close past the spot where we stood, carrying bushes and young trees along with it.(41)

Like the other dangers in Ballantyne's novel, the rock is external to the boys, just an accident of nature which they have to avoid. In the first chapter of *Lord of the Flies* the three boys happily push a large rock because it is there and asking to be pushed. Even so, the damage it inflicts on the forest is awesome and Golding's simile for its progress, ominous:

> ... the forest further down shook as with the passage of an enraged monster ...(37)

We return to the rock near the end when the symbolic Roger pushes one on to Piggy 'with a sense of delirious abandonment'(222) and when the savages try to force Ralph out of his hiding place:

> ... the earth jumped and began to shake steadily ... the whole thicket bent and the roots screamed as they came out of the earth together.(238)

What begins as a jolly adventure ends as an expression of the shattering of Ralph's world.

The first chapter ends with Jack's failure to 'stick' the piglet, despite encouragement from Ralph and Simon. The 'enormity of the knife descending'(41) prevents them from acting. The pressures of civilisation are still too prominent. As the cover of glamour and adventure is torn aside, as the inhibitions fostered by civilised society disappear, then both the pig and Piggy are doomed and the knife descends with ever-increasing freedom.

Foreshadowing devices are prominent in the second chapter and the gap between present jollity and future terror begins to shorten. Golding has remarked, in his essay, 'Crosses':

It has become a commonplace of this century that a random selection of people can inflict utter cruelty on one another. . . .[51]

and this chapter commences by balancing the sane, procedural movements of Ralph against the atavistic impulses already apparent in Jack. Ralph tries to adopt civilised procedures he remembers from school, trying to order the conditions on the island into a meaningful whole, insisting that the island society must have hunters, a fire, and rules:

> Jack was on his feet.
> 'We'll have rules!' he cried excitedly. 'Lots of rules! Then when anyone breaks 'em—'
> 'Whee-oh!'
> 'Wacco!'
> 'Bong!'
> 'Doink!'(44)

The 'Bong' has become as important as the rules. This is 'fun' violence, like the 'mock' fight, but the line between this and the real violence of survival is thinning. The boys, in their excitement, list other island adventure novels—*Treasure Island*; *Swallows and Amazons*; *The Coral Island*—but their dream-world is quickly punctured when the small boy with the mulberry-coloured birthmark introduces an alien element, the 'beastie'. The term 'beast' is to be much reiterated through this novel and manifold interpretations are to accrue to it. Here the small boy seems to have mistaken the large tree-creepers for snakes, apparently an ironic comment on the notion that every Eden must have its serpent. Yet the very presence of night-beasts in the dreams of the boys suggests a far remove from Arthur Ransome, and one reality of the 'beastie' is to be made clear before this chapter ends. One of the most pathetic aspects of both the reality of the boys and their fabulistic roles as frightened and confused humankind is their insistence on seeking the beast everywhere but in the place of its origin, the human heart. Adults can comfort children after nightmares but in a situation where no adults are present and where the nightmares are made to indicate the terrible limitations of adult knowledge no such comfort can emerge. Already Ralph's repetition, '... I tell you there isn't a beast'(48), betrays uncertainty.

The foreshadowing involved in this initial reference is then taken up and deepened with the fire and its aftermath. The original aim of the boys is to use the fire as a smoke signal. To the rationality of Ralph and Piggy it is essential that the fire is maintained to ensure rescue. It is their foremost symbol of safety but it also quickly becomes a promoter of conflict when Jack and the hunters, giving increasing rein to their savage instincts in pursuing the pigs, fail to maintain it. Even at this initial stage the mention of a fire breaks up the assembly. Jack takes up the suggestion, calls to the rest to follow him, and Ralph's further words are unheeded. Piggy remarks scornfully:

'Acting like a crowd of kids!'

Linked inextricably to the adult world, he moves after them 'with the martyred expression of a parent who has to keep up with the senseless ebullience of the children'(50), and he is, significantly, the only one to keep an eye on the conch.

Faced with the difficulty of lighting a fire, they grab Piggy's spectacles, the emblem of his braininess, and use them to start a flame. This seems reasonable since they are using one link with the adult world to foster another, their signal; but fire has other, quite different, subconscious associations, notably with all-consuming passions. It is a supreme irony that the spectacles, emblem of a 'civilised' intelligence, should become linked to the fire which comes, as much as the beast, to stand for that atavism so rampant by the end of the novel. The more sinister associations of the fire are fostered by Jack's assertion that the conch, the would-be symbol of order, does not 'count' on the mountain, the location of the fire. The futility of Jack's famous statement moments later is thus immediately clear:

'I agree with Ralph. We've got to have rules and obey them. After all, we're not savages. We're English, and the English are best at everything. So we've got to do the right things.'(55)

An early statement by Peterkin in *The Coral Island* quickly comes to mind:

'We've got an island all to ourselves. We'll take possession in the name of the king; we'll go and enter the service of its black inhabitants. Of course, we'll rise, naturally, to the top of affairs. White men always do in savage countries.'(15)

Public school jingoism already seems hideously out of place in *Lord of the Flies* because of Golding's ominous arrangement of his 'signs' (conch, snake, fire) and because, moments later, the hunters become closely associated with the fire. If the fire is first a rational but false symbol of safety and then, dominantly, an irrational but true symbol of destruction then it exactly parallels the symbolic use of the hunters who offer first a hope of sustenance and then a foreshadowing of disaster in their concern with killing rather than cooking. They are the savages who rise to power on the wings of passion.

Golding brilliantly unites these signs by showing the unintentional but inevitable spread of the fire to the forest; the useless destruction of much valuable wood and food. As the fire spreads Golding adroitly shifts similes to make its spreading illustrate the larger movement of the fable. First it is compared to a relatively harmless beast:

> The squirrel leapt on the wings of the wind and clung to another standing tree, eating downwards. Beneath the dark canopy of leaves and smoke the fire laid hold on the forest and began to gnaw.

The verb 'gnaw' prepares for the change into a more predatory creature:

> The flames, as though they were a kind of wild life, crept as a jaguar creeps on its belly toward a line of birch-like saplings that fledged an outcrop of the pink rock.(57)

The passion developing among the boys is to undergo a similar progress and its results are foreshadowed in the death, by fire, of the small boy with the mulberry-coloured birthmark. As his disappearance is apprehended by Piggy, so the fire intensifies:

> Tall swathes of creepers rose for a moment into view, agonised, and went down again. The little boys screamed at them.
> 'Snakes! Snakes! Look at the snakes!'(60)

The 'beastie', the idea of whose existence is uneasily ridiculed by the older boys, has claimed its first victim. The emotional upheaval signified by the fire, the evil power signified by the 'snake', has, as he had himself feared, 'eaten' the small boy. Although the fire does die out, the horror it suggests never can.

As we read through the novel we become aware of the care which Golding takes, at the start of each chapter, to suggest the 'progression' of the fable. The third chapter opens with Jack, and the passing of a period of time from the end of the previous chapter, overtly recognised in the increased length of his hair, is substantiated by our awareness of a change in his behaviour. He is hunting, but in terms which link him both to a savage and to a beast:

> He closed his eyes, raised his head and breathed in gently with flared nostrils, assessing the current of warm air for information.(61)

His behaviour is like that of Lok in Golding's second novel, *The Inheritors*:

> Lok's nose opened automatically and sampled the complex of odours that came with the mist.
> He cupped his hands over his nostrils and examined the trapped air. Eyes shut, straining attention, he concentrated on the touch of the warming air, seemed for a moment on the very brink of revelation.[52]

Yet, whereas Lok's behaviour is described warm-heartedly and made a part of his hard yet sensible association with nature, Jack's is clearly given to us as a reversion. It seems reasonable, in his predicament, to go hunting for food, but his 'motives' are suspect. We see that his eyes are 'nearly mad' in their frustration at wanting to find the pig. A little later we are told that they took on an 'opaque, mad look'(48). Moreover, while Golding wrote *The Inheritors* to counter H. G. Wells's suggestion that Neanderthal men were little more than apes, Jack's increasing bestiality links him with this very creature:

> ... for a minute [he] became less a hunter than a furtive thing, ape-like among the tangle of trees.(62)

While Jack grows to fit the role of principal savage, he is contrasted with the futile attempts to maintain the ordered society on the beach. Shelters are being built but few will work for any length of time. Communal work, like the voting, is a toy of which the boys quickly tire. Ralph angrily refers to the emptiness of talk at assemblies and berates Jack for wasting time chasing the pigs. The clash between the two provokes Simon into suggesting that the island may not be 'good' and the 'beastie' may be real and the authority of this is enhanced by Jack's momentary flash of insight which tells him that there may be a beast hunting him in the jungle. Ironically, he then suggests that the hunters paint their faces, ostensibly as a means of camouflaging themselves from the pigs. To Ralph Rover, in *The Coral Island*, the abominations of the cannibals are horrifyingly signposted by their painted faces:

> In ten minutes the canoe returned, bringing the other chief, who certainly presented a most extraordinary appearance, having painted one half of his face red and the other half yellow, besides ornamenting it with various designs in black ... (223-4)

(Jack uses red and white clay and charcoal). In *Lord of the Flies*, since pig and man are linked through beast imagery, camouflage against the pigs must involve a disguise against man's own nature at the same time as it presents the reader with an external sign of internal regressions. The white boys and the cannibals, bitter foes in Ballantyne's novel, now coalesce. In the next chapter, Jack's painting of his face widens the gap between himself and a Ralph still clinging to his original ideas of rules and work, two important elements of Ballantyne's nineteenth-century ethic.

The chapter ends with our first extended view of Simon. Ironically, Ralph had at first assumed him to be 'delightfully gay and wicked'(70), perhaps the 'devil' that Ralph was not; but our view of him here prepares us for the opposite of a 'devil'; Golding himself uses the term 'Christ-figure'.[53] Yet both terms suggest a welter of Christian symbolism quite inappropriate to the tenor of this novel. Simon is 'odd' and isolated. His isolation is rather like that of Jack at this chapter's opening:

> He looked over his shoulder as Jack had done at the close ways behind him and glanced swiftly round to confirm that he was utterly alone. For a moment his movements were almost furtive.(71–2)

Two points in this section, however, serve to contrast him with Jack. In the first place he makes a Christ-like gesture and reaches down fruit from the high branches to feed the littluns. Without intruding theological speculations, we are meant to see an alternative to Jack's atavism, that simple charity which binds a group together. To call Simon a 'Christ-figure' in this sense does not mean that we have to see his retreat to a hiding-place as a sojourn in the wilderness or an indication of sainthood, but as an attempt to understand mankind, whom he loves and wishes to help. Like the deaf-mute at the beginning of Melville's *The Confidence Man*, he offers a means to viable human relationships which mankind rejects. It embraces instead the atavism of Jack, which creates only a mob action where mutual understanding is impossible. The community on the boat-shaped island, like that on Melville's steamboat *Fidèle*, sails into the dark.

Secondly, Simon does have an intuitive perception of man's condition far beyond that of the others and this is marvellously evoked in these few pages. Ian Gregor and Mark Kinkead-Weekes[54] have pointed out how the nature described here is beautiful, but alien to man:

> Tall trunks bore unexpected pale flowers all the way up to the dark canopy where life went on clamorously.(71)

Since Simon is alone and, we are told, has 'cocked a critical ear at the

THE TEXT

sounds of the island'(72), we must accept that the description given here is what *Simon* sees and hears, not coloured by mood now, as with Ralph or Jack, but accepted whole and for what it is, something foreign to man which cannot control, or even respond to, his mistakes. Simon's view of nature, as later of man, is one of understanding and acceptance. Ralph wanted to light the candle-buds, Jack to cut and eat them, but Simon just *sees* them:

> The candle-buds stirred. Their green sepals drew back a little and the white tops of the flowers rose delicately to meet the open air.(72)

Simon is a 'visionary' when compared to the others, but his function is also as an interpreter for the readers, that figure who is closest to Golding's own view and who can suggest where the other boys are going terribly wrong.

The fourth chapter then begins with a continued view of nature:

> The first rhythm that they became used to was the slow swing from dawn to quick dusk.(73)

Time is passing and the boys are trying to attune themselves to the ways in which this happens on the island. The natural rhythms are, however, coloured by their fears. Morning is menaced by the heat of the afternoon; the cool of evening menaced by the coming darkness which brings night-fears. Attunement is limited by an attempted adherence to work and by the continuing fears of the littluns. Brutality is coming closer to the surface, though still held in check by memories of civilised order. Maurice, larking about, inadvertently kicks sand into Percival's eye and hurries guiltily away:

> At the back of his mind formed the uncertain outlines of an excuse ...(76)

and Roger, throwing stones at Henry, cannot bring himself to hit him:

> Round the squatting child was the protection of parents and school and policemen and the law.(78)

Yet it is with the small Henry that we become aware of a counter-movement to these civilised checks. He is down at the shore watching the movement of some tiny transparencies and becomes absorbed in shifting the sand around so that he can order these transparencies into certain patterns of behaviour. This is reminiscent of Richard Hughes, but *Lord of the Flies* is not a post-Freudian novel about children, concentrating imaginatively on a strictly-detailed account of the workings of a child's mind. We are to hear little of Henry after this. The real relevance of this episode seems to lie in its latent brutality and its foreshadowing power. Henry controls the transparencies:

> He became absorbed beyond mere happiness as he felt himself exercising control over living things.(77)

Ironically, Henry, who is the victim of Roger's stone-throwing, also points the way to the later Roger who 'sat still, assimilating the possibilities of irresponsible authority'. While throwing the stones Roger can hide his body behind a tree, but not his memory of laws and codes of conduct. Then he meets up with Jack who paints his face and presents both of them with a 'disguise' which liberates both body and memory. When Jack looks in a pool he sees, not himself, but 'an awesome stranger' and immediately this leads him to 'appall' his comrades and caper with a 'bloodthirsty snarling'. The mask becomes 'a thing on its own, behind which Jack hid, liberated from shame and self-consciousness'(80). In Freudian terms, the Egos of Jack, Roger and, by extension, many of the others, are becoming liberated from the controlling memories of the Super-Egos and thus yielding themselves to the dominance of the Ids, the primitive lusts located in the unconscious.

This movement is contrasted with the unchanging state of Piggy, a state which even Ralph is beginning to see as rather absurd. Piggy worries over practical matters, such as the making of a sun-dial, without imagination, and his physical presence increasingly posits him as a potential victim. His asthma remains; he refuses to go naked; his hair does not grow. Ralph finds him ridiculous yet shares enough of his attention to regulations to be appalled when the hunters allow the fire to go out, thus missing a ship on the horizon. As they stand in the misery of disappointment they hear the first ritual chants, chants which grow in volume and frequency later in the novel:

> '*Kill the pig. Cut her throat. Spill her blood.*'(86)

The real violence inherent in the chant coincides with the gross betrayal of the original rules and with the development in Jack of that knowledge first dimly perceived by Henry:

> His mind was crowded with memories; memories of the knowledge that had come to them when they closed in on the struggling pig,

knowledge that they had outwitted a living thing, imposed their will upon it, taken away its life like a long satisfying drink.(88)

Knowledge enormous makes savages of them but, without their realising it, it is a knowledge of the depths of human bestiality. In *The Coral Island* the boys do not always seem sure why they kill the pigs, but utilitarianism is paramount. Golding takes up the minuscule limits of the underlying passions that might be involved in the killing and makes them much more prominent. The pigs are sacrificed to the Id-power which is rapidly growing on the island. On the mountain irreparable breaches are created. Ralph rejects Jack's supposedly magnanimous apology and Jack transfers his aggression from the pig to Piggy. Atavism turns on weak common-sense and moves a long step back from civilisation by smashing one of the lenses in Piggy's spectacles.

The limitations of the fable

The danger of a closely-detailed critical study such as this is that it finds so much to admire that flaws are often happily forgotten. A pause will be useful in order to see how, if Golding manœuvres so many aspects of the fable so brilliantly, he also points to its major limitations.

The pitfalls facing a fabulist seem clear enough: a tendency to limit characters to cardboard abstractions; so great a removal from the details of real life as to seem cloyingly self-indulgent; a reduction of the fictional material to the barest rudimentary diagram (the truth must not be missed!); the loading of character or detail with symbolic weights which merely crush them out of all shape. Golding's particular trap is none of these in isolation or extent, though it partakes of all of them. In 'Fable' Golding insists that:

> The point of the fable under imaginative consideration does not become more real than the real world, it shoves the real world on one side.[55]

As we have already seen, the world of *Lord of the Flies* is credible, tangible, various, fascinating; in every way real. But he also says, of the method of the fabulist:

> Arranging his signs as he does, he reaches, not profundity on many

levels, but what you would expect from signs, that is overt significance.⁵⁶

Again, as we have seen, Golding arranges his signs very carefully and they are overt. They are, however, embedded firmly in the 'real' world of the fable and cannot be separated from its ironies and symbols. Like those of Lear's Fool, the points are subtly made and, like Lear, we have to open our eyes and hearts very wide. This means that the overtness of the signs ought to depend on the work which we, the readers, do to comprehend them. This we achieve only through immersion in the fictional world and the appeal of the consistency of that world to our imaginations. Time and again in this novel Golding fails to allow us that immersion. Towards the end of chapter three the widening gap between Ralph and Jack has been made quite clear through the signs surrounding each figure, but Golding cannot resist the extra-overt 'explanation':

> They walked along, two continents of experience and feeling, unable to communicate.(70)

The relative positions of Roger and Henry on the sea-shore and the human limitations which each illustrates do not need the fussy explication of the author:

> Roger's arm was conditioned by a civilisation that knew nothing of him and was in ruins.(78)

When Jack and his hunters allow the fire to go out, Ralph, wildly angry, is waiting for them on the mountain:

> The two boys faced each other. There was the brilliant world of hunting, tactics, fierce exhilaration, skill; and there was the world of longing and baffled common-sense.(89)

Haven't we already been able to see the growth of the different 'camps' to which Jack and Ralph belong, and part of the symbolic distinctions made between them? Doesn't the authorial intrusion spoil the narrative perspective; dull the ironies; diffuse the tension?

Critics who complain of the symbolic weight Simon has to bear often forget that it is they who dumped it upon him, but, even so, Golding does keep him out of the narrative for awkwardly long spells, resulting in blatancy when he does appear. In chapter six some of the boys go searching for the beast. Simon, who has been absent from our attention for some time, suddenly has a vision of the truth:

However Simon thought of the beast, there rose before his inward
sight the picture of a human at once heroic and sick.(128)

He senses now what he will see later but this momentary glimpse of the
truth is too sudden for the reader. A little later he appears by the side of
Ralph, who is staring out to sea, and assures him, 'You'll get back to
where you came from'(137). Simon is a visionary and so must be more
shadowy than the others, but at the end of chapter three his symbolic
role is presented by means of carefully chosen realistic detail. He *is*
a boy on the island and at moments such as those quoted above, he
ceases to be a boy and becomes a puppet whose jerky movements are
dictated by the needs of the fable.

Golding points out, in 'Fable':

. . . there are many places I am sure where the fable splits at the seams
and I would like to think that if this is so, the splits do not rise from
ineptitude or deficiency but from a plenitude of imagination.[57]

He is wrong. The splits occur from a lack of faith either in the capacity
of his imagination or that of his readers, and they sometimes threaten to
upturn both the consistency of the fable and the commitment of the
reader's imaginative response.

Beasts and violence

Chapter five begins with Ralph and helps to make clear that, although
the novel is basically an inverted *Coral Island*, although its main impetus
is toward the delineation of a community and the various forces con-
tending within that community, it is a book with a hero, Ralph, who,
although the novel is not a first-person narrative, is the learner, the 'eye'
in more important ways than Ralph Rover of the earlier book. Life on
the island, he has discovered, is not idyllic:

He found himself understanding the wearisomeness of this life, where
every path was an improvisation and a considerable part of one's
working life was spent watching one's feet.(95)

He is growing up to see the dirt on the boys' clothes, to ask himself
difficult questions about the perception of reality:

If faces were different when lit from above or below—what was a face? What was anything?(97)

The fumbling growth of his awareness is contrasted with Piggy's limited wisdom. In the assembly Piggy's 'truth' is ironically given to the reader while he [Piggy] is completely unaware of it:

> 'I know there isn't no beast—not with claws and all that, I mean—but I know there isn't no fear, either.'(105)

Like Mark Twain in *Huckleberry Finn*, Golding is aware of the force of a double negative to suggest a positive. The difference between what Piggy *means* and what he *says* is total.

Most of the chapter is taken up with a discussion of the 'beast'. Although the older boys still try desperately to deny its existence, they do discuss the possibility of its residing in the forest. Like the early Puritan settlers in America, they try for locations of evil outside themselves; dark domains away from the comfort of the camp. Works such as Hawthorne's 'Young Goodman Brown' and Arthur Miller's *The Crucible* ruthlessly use the symbolic forest area as a means of locating evil where it belongs, within man. Similarly, Golding brings the darkness on the island inexorably nearer to its real source. Even Piggy, without understanding its implications, perceives the truth:

> '. . . there isn't no fear . . .
> Unless we get frightened of people'(105)

and an ordinary event takes on a great foreshadowing irony when a littlun claims to have seen something 'big and horrid'(106) moving among the trees at night. Simon, amid derision, admits that he was taking a nocturnal walk. On one level the identification is absurd because Simon is destroyed by the 'beast' when he discovers its true identity, but on another it is quite right because everyone on the island is the beast; it is a collective responsibility. A further attempt to externalise the evil in the sea is greeted by an absurd argument which, to Ralph, 'seemed the breaking up of sanity'(110).

Then Simon, timidly, puts forward his view:

> '. . . maybe there is a beast . . . maybe it's only us.'
> Simon became inarticulate in his effort to express mankind's essential illness. Inspiration came to him.
> 'What's the dirtiest thing there is?'

THE TEXT

As an answer Jack dropped into the incomprehending silence that followed it the one crude expressive syllable.(110-11)

The syllable is, of course, 'shit', and everybody laughs. Golding is again arranging his signs cleverly, though in a more academic way than is the custom with this novel. The chapter opened with Ralph realising how dirty the boys, including himself, are and he later berates the littluns for defecating near the fruit because that's 'dirty'. Now physical unpleasantness becomes expressive of spiritual ugliness. The Hebrew word, 'Beelzebub', though it means literally 'lord of flies', might be rendered in English as 'lord of dung', that substance around which flies gather. Jack's expressive syllable, which is at once both an answer to Simon and a derision of Simon's fumbling attempt to find a solution, becomes in itself a comprehensive definition of man's frailty. The lord of dung exists within the boys, where excrement is formed, and finds his physical expression in the dirt-encrusted bodies of those at the assembly.

When, despite the derision, there is a vote in favour of the existence of ghosts, Ralph feels that

The world, that understandable and lawful world, was slipping away.

and this is immediately confirmed when Jack refutes the rules in violent incantation:

'Bollocks to the rules! We're strong—we hunt! If there's a beast, we'll hunt it down. We'll close in and beat and beat and beat—!'(114)

The Opies make it clear that, until the age of fourteen or so, children place a much higher value on the rites of their peers than on those of adults close to them. After that age they quickly become involved in family, adult traditions. Children naturally tend to practise charms and rites because of their involvement with the mysterious:

... they appear to have an innate awareness that there is more to the ordering of fate than appears on the surface. And yet other practices and beliefs are undoubtedly so taken for granted that it is not appreciated that the custom or belief is in fact superstitious. It must, after all, be borne in mind that the children here under observation are only at the stage of mental development sometimes ascribed to a savage tribe, whom anthropologists are not at all surprised to find dominated by superstition.[58]

Golding's boys are under fourteen and in their increasing adherence to incantation and superstition they become totally removed from responsibility to rules and retreat to primal savagery. In the Opies' terms any discarding of these superstitions is impossible because the domestic traditions associated with the family, the adult society, are present only in the weak figure of Piggy, who denies the possibility of ghosts:

> "'Cos things wouldn't make sense. Houses an' streets, an'—TV— they wouldn't work.'(115)

Piggy's position may remind us of an earlier novella which several commentators have seen as a possible influence on Golding's book, Joseph Conrad's *Heart of Darkness*. After the narrator, Marlow, has sailed up the Congo, seen Kurtz, and understood from seeing him the horror of which man is capable, the abyss which yawns beneath all men if they dare to look into it, he returns to Brussels, largely despising the houses and streets and dull daily round, the paraphernalia of a civilised society which does not recognise the existence of a heart of darkness. Marlow has seen it and, in a sense, has the best (or worst) of both worlds. To some small degree Ralph's position at the end of this novel is analagous to Marlow's; he has recognised the full horror of the atavism let loose on the island and at the same time, as his weeping may suggest, an awareness of that world represented by the cruiser. Piggy, on the other hand, is like a citizen of Brussels who is thrust into the world of the Congo and tries to pretend that there is no jungle, tries to maintain stability through memories of the houses and streets. Listening to the chanting boys, whose incantations have worked away to a wordless rhythm, Piggy and Ralph wish that grown-ups would appear:

> 'They ain't afraid of the dark. They'd meet and have tea and discuss, ... 'If only they could get a message to us ... If only they could send us something grown-up ... a sign or something.'(117)

In the next chapter they *do* send a sign but at the end of chapter five we are given a terrifying hint of the limitations of that sign. An unearthly wail is set up from another direction. It comes from Percival, whose repetition of his name and address has turned into an 'inarticulate gibbering'(117). He had been taught this recitation by his parents in case he ever got lost. He is now lost beyond redemption and his incantation becomes as meaningless as the wordless rhythm from the boys on the beach. This is a sign from the adults which is now, in this society, of no use, and it is as awful in its incomprehensibility as the yells of savages.

Chapter six, then, opens with a sign from the grown-ups. From a battle fought at ten miles height a dead airman drops to the island by parachute and is to be feared by the boys as a 'beast'. He is a victim of hate, of the cruelty of the human heart and also a symbol of that cruelty. The 'beast' is a dead man from a dying world, a world torn apart by war. The boys, of course, see him as an external evil and we might be tempted to see the world which sends him as an external force which surrounds the boys menacingly. Yet we have already discussed the island society as a microcosm, which implies that this society reproduces the forces which are rampant in the macrocosm, the larger world. By this connection civilisation is seen to be as atavistic as the 'primitive' island tribe and the trappings of safety, for which Piggy longs, are really useless. The airman has a parachute, a sophisticated safety apparatus, yet all it can do is rob the man even of his dignity in death:

> When the breeze blew, the lines would strain taut, and some accident of this pull lifted the head and chest upright so that the figure seemed to peer across the brow of the mountain.(119)

He is like Percival. Neither is served by their civilised equipment. Man's reliance on society's offerings here turn him into a figure as puppet-like as those who blindly obey Jack. The helplessness of the human predicament is mirrored by Eric's view of woodlice scurrying frantically away from the flames. In the first chapter, when Jack, Ralph and Simon look down from the mountain, the boys on the beach look like insects and the connection is continued here. Since we have discussed the fire as a symbol of an internal condition which manifests itself in shocking violence, it is hardly a long step to feeling that the small boy with the mulberry-coloured birthmark must also have scurried, insect-like, in a vain effort to avoid the flames. This scene is very reminiscent of one near the end of Ernest Hemingway's *A Farewell to Arms*,[59] where Frederick Henry considers man's situation as like that of insects on a log he once thrust into a camp-fire. He could play God by lifting it out again, but this makes him realise that any higher power must be as capricious as he. This specifically relates to the futility of Catherine Barkley's death. For both writers man can find no help in nature or the idea of a higher power. Hemingway can, in much of his fiction, suggest the possibility of individual courage (Christ's death didn't change anything but he was 'pretty good in there')[60] through the manner in which a person faces the inevitable loss and destruction the world forces upon him. In Golding's world no such view is possible. We are given, instead, a nature permanently alien to man:

> Then the sleeping leviathan breathed out, the waters rose, the weed streamed, and the water boiled over the table rock with a roar.(131)

and a group of panicky boys off to find and kill a dead man.

It is possible to discuss the second half of the novel more briefly since the signs have been clearly set out and a development started which now has an inevitable movement. The next three chapters illustrate the long movement from fun and games to hysterical ritual and brutality. Ralph has gained some objectivity and can see the boys as grubby like himself (Piggy, with the olympian view of a weary adult, never sees himself as one of the boys). His growing perception is enforced by his sense of man's isolation in nature:

> ... but here, faced by the brute obtuseness of the ocean, the rules of division, one was clamped down, one was helpless, one was condemned...(137)

Yet his objectivity can, like that of the naval officer, be too narrow. Ralph's scornful view, later, of the savages as just, 'boys armed with sticks'(116), is to widen yet further the rift between himself and Jack.

When Robert acts the beast, the violence of the 'game' surprises and frightens him. Ralph tries to keep it on the level of 'play' by linking it with earlier games in the secure world:

> 'I got jolly badly hurt at rugger once.'(142)

but rugger, like the game of tag, has strict rules. It is played in games time and then there is a return to the rules of the working world. Here there is nowhere to return to and so the game, unable to end, turns into something else. At the moment everybody laughs at Jack's suggestion that they practise on a littlun; later they use two biguns, Simon and Piggy. Ralph's nostalgia for Dartmoor and the comfort of an ordered world is totally futile when placed against these 'games' and the first sight of the 'beast'. The comfortable world is in tatters and, as representative of a ruined macrocosm, the dead airman presents them with the ruins of a face. They see the airman, indistinctly, as 'something like a great ape'(114), the creature associated earlier with Jack who also represents the ruin of civilised possibilities.

In view of the gathering definitions of the beast, Jack's tearful decision after a row with Ralph:

'I'm not going to play any longer.'(158)

is horridly ironic. It has been clear for some time that the element of play is being transformed into ritualised hysteria without restraint. Jack's statement, which has, like most of the boys' statements, a far larger meaning than they can know, represents the final shift, the plummet into the abyss, and it is soon followed by the killing of the sow.

The peace and harmony of the pigs is rudely shattered by the humans. The equivalent scene in *The Coral Island* is presented with some flippancy as Peterkin stabs the sow:

> Nay, so vigorously was it done that the spear went in at one side and came out at the other!
> 'Oh, Peterkin!' said I, going up to him, 'what have you done?'
> 'Done? I've killed their great-great-grandmother that's all,' said he, looking with a somewhat awestruck expression at the transfixed animal.(125)

Any horror we may feel at the killing, any intimation we may have of hidden emotions being brought into play, is obviated by focusing our attention on the boys, thus reducing the pigs to amusing objects. Golding does not try to humanise the pigs: they are as alien as the rest of the natural surround:

> She was black and pink; and the great bladder of her belly was fringed with a row of piglets that slept or burrowed and squeaked. . . .(166)

but he does give us, momentarily, a view of the killing through the sow's eyes, as weirdly-coloured, shrieking invaders from another world hurl themselves upon her. Moreover, the language of this scene is universes removed from Ballantyne's uninspired jogtrot.

> The afternoon wore on, hazy and dreadful with damp heat; the sow staggered her way ahead of them, bleeding and mad, and the hunters followed, wedded to her in lust, excited by the long chase and the dropped blood.

The prose is charged with the shock of a new emotion: 'wedded', 'lust', 'excited':

> The sow collapsed under them and they were heavy and fulfilled upon her.(168)

Perhaps E. L. Epstein's reference to an 'Oedipal wedding night' is an intrusion of terminology which both literary critics and psychologists would find difficult to sustain, but clearly a kind of unconscious recognition is shown here, an entry into an experience much greater than just the killing of the sow. The language of the sex act may represent the power over the female principle first recognised in early adolescence but, in terms of the fable, the killing is expressed in sexual terms to indicate a completion of the release of tremendous physical power which is to override all else. The 'play', truly, has ended.

They leave the pig's head as propitiation to the beast. Covered in flies it becomes the most literal sign of Beelzebub. The Philistine deity exactly suits the pagan uprising so vividly enacted when the sow dies. Unknown to Jack and the hunters, Simon is in his covert staring directly at the head. Golding felt that this may be one point in the novel where the bare bones of the thesis stick in an ungainly fashion through the flesh of the novel, but, in fact, the whole episode of Simon's final confirmation of his theories is brilliantly achieved. Like other crucial scenes in this novel, it works fully on both realistic and symbolic levels. Since Simon is, presumably, an epileptic, suffering from what the ancients called 'the sacred disease', then it is right that, suffering from heat, worry and fear, he should have his sensations sufficiently disturbed to hallucinate a monologue from the pig's head. Symbolically, this may well be the central sign of the book, since it welds together other aspects of the beast. It is the beast, the head of the beast, the offering to the beast, left by the boys whose bestiality is marked by the head on a stick. The head becomes an external sign of Simon's recognition of his own state and that of the whole world. Adult life is no longer comforting, but capable of 'infinite cynicism'. Simon's head becomes the pig's head; the flies drink his sweat. The head insists on the rightness of this:

> 'You knew, didn't you? I'm part of you? Close, close, close! I'm the reason why it's no go?'(177)

When Simon feels himself falling, it is as much into the black pit of his own mouth as that of the pig. At one point in *Heart of Darkness* the abyss yawning before Kurtz and Marlow is pointed by the image of Kurtz's mouth, and Marlow, peering into the darkness, sees the same depths of depravity as Simon, 'the memory of gratified and monstrous passions'. To both comes that 'ancient, inescapable recognition' of man's innate depravity. The Lord of the Flies insists that they are all going to have 'fun', but the word which began by linking this novel to the world of Arthur Ransome has now become the Devil's talk and can mean only one thing.

Our view of Simon is balanced, in chapter eight, by a view of Ralph and Piggy still trying to blame the symptom, Jack, rather than the cause. Ralph does give an indication of why he is to be saved:

> 'I'd like to put on war-paint and be a savage. But we must keep the fire burning. The fire's the most important thing on the island, because, because—'(175–6)

Marlow, an intelligent, sensitive observer, has a similar recognition of the attractions of atavism. Steaming up the Congo he sees naked savages dancing on the shore and is 'thrilled' to feel his 'remote kinship'[61] with them. Why doesn't he get off the boat and join the dance?

> 'I had to watch the steering, and circumvent those snags, and get the tin-pot along by hook or by crook. There was surface-truth enough in these things to save a wiser man.'[62]

Ralph's adherence to the 'surface-truth' of the fire helps to save him because, unlike Piggy, he does have glimpses of Simon's 'deep' truth. When Simon has been killed by the mob Piggy refuses to admit that murder has been committed. Stubbornly, he insists that it was all an accident but Ralph, who senses the attraction/repulsion of ritual solidarity, nonetheless sees the bloodletting for what it is. If there is feverish excitement in his voice, there is also loathing. As the terror increases Ralph becomes more confused about the 'goodness' of the fire but clings tenaciously to his blurred memories of its usefulness while Piggy's solemn consideration of the problems of writing to his auntie continues to highlight the differences between them.

This follows the contrast between Simon and Jack in chapter nine, a contrast which can only lead to Simon's death. Following his 'interview' with the pig's head, Simon goes up the mountain, walking 'with a sort of glum determination like an old man'(180). This is not the uncomprehending 'adult' position adopted by Piggy but a mature acceptance of a responsibility for man's condition. Knowledge does not alter Simon's Christ-like stature, it enhances it. Despite the unpleasantness involved, he performs a great act of charity; he untangles the airman's body from the parachute harness. Like Donne he has discovered that 'no man is an island'. He *is* the dead airman (whose head is also encircled with flies) and only such a concrete acknowledgment of kinship will do.

Meanwhile, Jack is gathering greater power and thus increasing his bestiality:

> ... authority sat on his shoulder and chattered in his ear like an ape.(185)

As his bestiality increases so magic takes over from rationality. The storm provokes a ritual dance of propitiation. In mob action is safety. Even Ralph, who sees the gathering as demented, is strongly aware of the security it offers. Into this closed society stumbles Simon, a Messiah from the wilderness come to tell his people about themselves. Like all great truthtellers he is treated brutally by an uncomprehending community. In a terrifying scene he is killed. He is seen and referred to as 'the beast' while he is trying to tell them about the dead human being which they have been calling 'beast', and being torn to pieces by human beings who now appear to have teeth and claws. The emotional force of the description should not blind us to the ironies involved. The parallels between Simon and the airman are well worked out. Both are seen at this point as the beast. The airman is a member of the adult society, the macrocosm, killed by that world: Simon is a child, a member of the microcosm, killed by that world. The dead man is a sign from the adult world which Simon, bearing an adult responsibility, tries to communicate to the others. Finally, both are borne away by the neutral sea. The movement of Simon's body has already been discussed. The transparencies, over which Henry tried to wield power, escort his body to sea and though they have no connection with the human world they appear to treat the dead child much more tenderly than his fellows. By these 'accidental' means Golding creates an elegiac exit for the truth teller. Simon moves out to sea almost in the manner in which Horatio hoped the dead Hamlet would journey to his peace.

Chapters ten and eleven are motional chapters. The hunters sneak up to Ralph's area of the island and steal Piggy's spectacles which have been smashed beyond repair. In the attempted defence of these last vestiges of rationality, Piggy, Ralph and Samneric miss the enemy in the turmoil and end up fighting themselves. Confusion now covers the full extent of the island. The small band travel to Castle Rock to recover their property but, faced with the savages who were once small boys, they can find no viable mode of communication. All rules are violently denied. Piggy is killed, his body taken out to sea, and Roger, with a 'hangman's horror' (224) clinging to him, focalises the violence. There is no longer any questioning of the nature of authority, only an individual in the ritual pattern, regarded with superstitious dread by the rest of the tribe.

The sense of an ending

The final chapter of *Lord of the Flies* has provoked a good deal of critical controversy. Two major questions need to be discussed:

1. What do the last three pages mean? Are the boys saved? What powers are represented by the naval officer?
2. How successful is the ending artistically? Has Golding 'sold' the fable? Are the ironies too heavy-handed and glib?

Ralph keeps hoping some change will take place to ensure his safety, but he has learnt too much not to be aware of the absurdity of such a desire:

> These painted savages would go further and further. Then there was that indefinable connection between himself and Jack; who therefore would never let him alone; never.(226)

The connection is based on the knowledge that primitive societies, in order to survive, can allow the existence of only one leader; any pretender must be ruthlessly exterminated. Similarly, his attempt to fob off previous incidents as an 'accident' is made ludicrous by his stumbling upon the skull, the repository of dark responses:

> ... The skull regarded Ralph like one who knows all the answers and won't tell.(228)

He smashes it but the grin remains. He cannot erase the symbolism of the skull, the knowledge it brings. Nostalgia is also useless:

> Might it not be possible to walk boldly into the fort, say—'I've got pax', laugh lightly and sleep among the others? Pretend they were still boys, schoolboys who had said, 'Sir, yes Sir'—and worn caps? Daylight might have answered yes; but darkness and the horrors of death said no.(228)

The Opies, discussing 'truce terms', make the following note under *Pax*:

> The usual term in private schools and school stories, 'pax', is group dialect not regional dialect. Thus a 14-year-old prep. school girl in

1954: 'When life becomes too bad you shriek "Pax". Once you have uttered this magic word you are safe.'[63]

'Pax' is an archaic term, related to the past, to memory, to books. It is eminently a cry we might expect from one of Ballantyne's public-school prefects disguised as callow sailors.[64] Its use by Ralph is wholly ironic since it has no connection with the very real dialogue of Golding's boys or with the frightening 'game' of tag which dominates the chapter. Instead, Roger sharpens a stick at both ends. Ralph is to become a pig. Nightmares of falling and death are replaced by an equally grim daylight reality where Ralph is chased by a snake-like line of savages, and where the fire, which threw up the 'snakes' before, now consumes the forest at about the same rate as the 'snake' nears Ralph. These twin pursuers have almost caught him when he arrives at the beach to find the adult world puzzling at the chase.

Our first glimpse of the naval officer is almost of that motion-picture cavalryman who rescues a young woman and her children from savage Red Indians:

> It was a white-topped cap, and above the green shade of the peak was a crown, an anchor, gold foliage. He saw white drill, epaulettes, a revolver, a row of gilt buttons down the front of a uniform.(246)

James Gindin, in his excellent book, *Postwar British Fiction*, calls the last three pages of *Lord of the Flies* a 'gimmick'; indeed, this is Golding's own term. Professor Gindin suggests that the 'gimmick' works against the run of the fable, weakens or possibly invalidates the reference of meaning that Golding has already established through symbol and metaphor:

> Ralph and Piggy often appealed to adult sanity in their futile attempts to control their world but suddenly and inconsistently at the end of the novel, adult sanity really exists.[65]

This, he says, is a trick:

> A means of cutting down or softening the implications built up within the structure of the boys' society on the island.[66]

The 'gimmick', he maintains, forces us to face this question:

> If the adult world rescues the boys in *Lord of the Flies*, are the depravity and brutality of human nature so complete?[67]

The word 'gimmick' normally has a pejorative ring. It is a description of trickery employed by stage magicians or carnival hustlers. Yet Golding could hardly have meant it in this sense. Does it work for the fable? Does it enhance our understanding of the theme? Structurally it can be faulted on the grounds of clumsiness. Basically, Golding is using a device known as the *deus ex machina*, the god from a machine, a device particularly used by Euripides and involving a god-figure lowered by machinery on to the stage to unravel the intricacies of the plot and possibly rescue the hero. In current usage it refers to any artificially induced ending which suddenly resolves great difficulties. When Macheath is suddenly reprieved at the end of *The Threepenny Opera* we applaud, realising that Brecht has tongue firmly in cheek. Most serious writers do not risk such an arbitrary device.[68] In one sense its suddenness at the end of *Lord of the Flies* is right because the boys have been much too preoccupied with the 'game' to notice an approach from the sea. Even so, the brevity of the adults' appearance must be deplored. Aristotle, in his *Poetics*, argued that a dénouement should arise naturally from the events of the story. Golding's ending, though thematically appropriate, has too much of a 'tagged-on' look to be totally assimilated into the whole.

However, there are several points to be made in defence of the ending; points which would seem to weaken Professor Gindin's case. The double perspective has already been mentioned. We have seen the 'heart of darkness' working through the boys' actions, the officer sees only dirty, frightened little boys. His inability to recognise what has happened mirrors man's inability to recognise his own capacity for evil. The adult is as blind as the boys (except Simon and Ralph). This is rather like the ironic gap developed by Richard Hughes when his children are released from the pirate ship into the custody of Miss Louisa Dawson, a well-bred young lady:

> How difficult it was to imagine that these happy-looking creatures had been, for months together, in hourly danger of their lives. Why had they not died of fright? She was sure that she would have, or at least gone stark, staring, raving mad.[69]

A naïve adult adheres to the notion that children are innocents threatened by a hostile adult world and promptly inverts the truth. A new adult in the story, knowing nothing of previous activities, offers a fertile field for multiplying ironies, and Golding works hard at these. We have almost forgotten that we are dealing with children and thus are pulled up sharply by the officer's phrase, 'fun and games'; words which now mean something quite different to us. The officer's cheerful stupidity leads to one irony after another:

> 'We saw your smoke. What have you been doing? Having a war or something?'(247)

and it is inevitable that he trots out the same jingoism as Jack:

> 'I should have thought that a pack of British boys... would have been able to put up a better show than that...'(248)

This is a god from a machine who seems godlike to the boys. Yet he is an infernal god from a diabolic machine. We soon see his revolver and the two ratings with sub-machine guns, while the last object mentioned in the novel is the 'trim cruiser', an agent of war. Does adult society *rescue* the boys?[70] One dictionary defines 'rescue' as 'to free or deliver from confinement, violence, danger or evil'. 'Rescue' is possible in *The Coral Island*, where only external danger threatens, but not here. Man (in the boys) is wicked. Let's stop the silly game before someone else gets hurt. Let's get them into the ship and away. But away to what? Apparently to a world which still cannot recognise its own evil and is in the process of blowing itself to pieces: a world for which the dead airman was an appallingly apt emblem. The pattern is complete.

Ralph weeps and embarrasses the officer. He weeps for the 'darkness of man's heart' (248), as evident now to him as it has been to us, and also for 'the end of innocence' (248). Were the children ever innocent? They are never seen as remotely like the innocents of Rousseau or Wordsworth. Golding the schoolmaster has, from the beginning, seen them far too realistically to invoke that myth. In terms of the fable Ralph weeps in realising his 'fallen nature', the reason why he and all men perversely destroy themselves. Innocence is only ignorance. Ralph weeps for a world he thought existed. He cannot embrace the adult world as a security: he knows that it has too many intimate connections with the savage fury unleashed on the island. The end in weeping completes the inversion of *The Coral Island*, whose ending sparkles, like each episode of *The Avengers*, with the sense of a job well done.

Lord of the Flies has been a fantastically popular book, especially among students. In the United States it replaced *The Catcher in the Rye* as required hip-pocket reading. Some years ago, Francis E. Kearns and Luke M. Grande carried on a debate in *America* and *Commonweal* over the reasons for this.[71] Mr. Kearns suggested that a revival of the conservative spirit among college students might account for the popularity of a pessimistic view of human progress, and Brother Luke countered by suggesting that Golding focussed on a choice between good and evil and allowed hope to remain in the character of Ralph. The ability to weep should be the sign of a willing heart.

Certainly the students of the past decade have been prepared to take a sterner view of man than that contained within the subtle sentimentalities of Salinger's book, but their determination to end war and their insistence on the binding power of love to create a workable society would argue against their eager acceptance of a totally pessimistic novel. It does not seem to matter that Ralph is saved accidentally: the point is, he survives. It is in the character of Ralph that the prevailing darkness of the fable is mitigated. He begins by merely accepting that to hold the conch implies leadership of a rational kind. He leans on the conch as Jack tried to lean on his position as head chorister. The conch, at first, makes him speak with the authority of genuine leadership, but as the basic human conflicts begin to weigh upon his mind he becomes muddled, unsure, fumbling; no longer realistically aware of the values of the conch and the fire, although he has avoided the stasis of Piggy by trying to reason out their applicability:

> By now, Ralph had no self-consciousness in public thinking but would treat the day's decisions as though he were playing chess. The only trouble was that he would never be a very good chess player.(145)

As democracy dwindles in authority and is swamped by the emergent totalitarian power of Jack and his gang, Ralph is thrown back on his limited powers of reasoning and his ability to understand his relation to the growing darkness on the island. His thoughts are fumbling, lacking in coherence, but he does try. He begins by partly believing in the beast (a willingness to externalise evil in order to avoid responsibility) but the sacrifice of Simon propels him toward an awareness of guilt. Piggy's reliance on adult rationality crumbles when Ralph challenges him with their complicity in Simon's murder. Ralph ponders on the problems of human identity and, in the last chapter, realising that he is unable to stop the 'game', shoulders the burden of his knowledge. In Ralph, weeping, we have an ordinary, decent human being almost destroyed by forces he cannot control but who, through struggling to comprehend those forces, gains something approaching heroic stature. Perhaps the fable, in a small way, joins forces here with the *bildungsroman*, the novel of 'education'. With this 'education' he does survive. The world outside is still a black place, but the *bildungsroman* never suggests that a knowledge of man leads, in some fairy tale manner, to an abrupt change in the macrocosm. Pip's knowledge of himself, in *Great Expectations*, enables him to function much more lovingly as a human being, but Victorian society rolls on as before. With his 'education', Ralph may go back to society a saner, wiser individual: one of those who are prepared to stop the world reaching those stages at which it throws up the dead airman and the trim cruiser in the distance.

3. Select Bibliography

(Place of publication, London, except where otherwise specified)

A. Works by William Golding:

Novels
Lord of the Flies, 1954
The Inheritors, 1955
Pincher Martin, 1956
Free Fall, 1959
The Spire, 1964
The Pyramid, 1967

Drama
The Brass Butterfly, 1958

Prose
The Hot Gates, and Other Occasional Pieces, 1965

B. Works about William Golding:

[Essays marked with an asterisk may be found in William Nelson (ed.), *William Golding's Lord of the Flies. A Source Book* (New York, 1963.]

J. R. Baker, *William Golding* (New York, 1965)

Arthur T. Broes, 'The Two Worlds of William Golding', in *Lectures on Modern Novelists*, Carnegie Series in English, No. 7 (Pittsburgh, 1963), pp. 1–14.

C. B. Cox, 'Lord of the Flies', *Critical Quarterly*, II (1960), pp. 112–17.*

B. F. Dick, *William Golding* (New York, 1967).

Ralph Freedman, 'The New Realism: The Fancy of William Golding', *Perspective*, X (Summer–Autumn, 1958), pp. 118–28.*

J. J. Gindin, *Postwar British Fiction* (Berkeley and Los Angeles, 1962).

Luke M. Grande, 'The Appeal of Golding', *Commonweal*, LXXVII (January 25, 1963), pp. 457–9* (and Francis E. Kearns), 'An

Exchange of Views: "The Appeal of Golding"', *Commonweal*, LXXVII (22 February 1963), pp. 569–71.*

Martin Green, 'Distaste for the Contemporary', *Nation*, CXC (12 May 1960), pp. 451–4.*

Peter Green, 'The World of William Golding', *Transactions and Proceedings of the Royal Society of Literature*, 32 (1963), pp. 37–57.*

Mark Kinkead-Weekes and Ian Gregor, *William Golding: A Critical Study* (1967).

Leighton Hodson, *William Golding* (Edinburgh, 1969).

Samuel Hynes, *William Golding* (New York, 1964).

Francis E. Kearns, 'Salinger and Golding: Conflict on the Campus', *America*, CVIII (26 January 1963), pp. 136–39.* 'Golding Revisited', in *William Golding's Lord of the Flies. A Source Book* (ed. (Nelson), pp. 165–9.*

F. Kermode, *Puzzles and Epiphanies* (1962).

Millar Maclure, 'Allegories of Innocence', *Dalhousie Review*, XL (Summer, 1960), pp. 145–56.

Carl Niemeyer, 'The Coral Island Revisited', *College English*, XXII (January 1961), pp. 241–5.*

Bern Oldsey and Stanley Weintraub, *The Art of William Golding* (New York, 1965).

John Peter, 'The Fables of William Golding', *Kenyon Review*, XIX (Autumn, 1957), pp. 577–92.*

Claire Rosenfield, 'Men of a Smaller Growth: A Psychological Analysis of William Golding's *Lord of the Flies*', *Literature and Psychology*, XI (Autumn, 1961), pp. 93–6, 99–101.*

Henri A. Talon, *Le Mal dans l'oeuvre de William Golding* (Paris, 1966).

Margaret Walters, 'Two Fabulists: Golding and Camus', *Melbourne Critical Review*, IV (1961), pp. 18–29.*

C. Further Reading related to this study.

R. M. Ballantyne, *The Coral Island* (Edinburgh, 1857).

John Bunyan, *The Pilgrim's Progress* (1678).

F. R. de Chateaubriand, *The Genius of Christianity* (Paris, 1802).

James Fenimore Cooper, *The Deerslayer* (New York, 1841).

P. Coveney, *The Image of Childhood* (first published as *Poor Monkey*) (1957).

SELECT BIBLIOGRAPHY

Joseph Conrad, *Heart of Darkness* (1902).

Stephen Crane, *The Red Badge of Courage* (New York, 1895),

Daniel Defoe, *Robinson Crusoe* (1719).

Charles Dickens, *Oliver Twist* (1836–1837).
Great Expectations (1860–1861).

George Eliot, *The Mill on the Floss* (1860).

Sigmund Freud, *Three Essays on the Theory of Sexuality* (Leipzig and Vienna, 1905).

Ernest Hemingway, *Men Without Women* (New York, 1927). *A Farewell to Arms* (New York, 1929).

Richard Hughes, *A High Wind in Jamaica* (1929).

Henry James, *What Maisie Knew* (New York, 1897). *The Turn of the Screw* (New York, 1898).

Charles Kingsley, *Alton Locke* (1849).

William March (pseud.), *The Bad Seed* (New York, 1954).

James Vance Marshall, *Walkabout* (first published as *The Children*) (1959).

Herman Melville, *The Confidence-Man* (New York, 1857).

Arthur Miller, *The Crucible* (New York, 1953).

I. and P. Opie, *The Lore and Language of Schoolchildren* (Oxford, 1959).

George Orwell, *Animal Farm* (1945).

Arthur Ransome, *Swallows and Amazons* (1930).

J.-J. Rousseau, *Émile* (Paris, 1762).

J. D. Salinger, *The Catcher in the Rye* (New York, 1951).

Alan Sillitoe, *Saturday Night and Sunday Morning* (1958). *Key to the Door* (1961).

Mark Twain, *Tom Sawyer* (New York, 1876). *Huckleberry Finn* (New York, 1885).

I. Watt, *The Rise of the Novel* (1957).

Notes

1. John Peter, 'The Fables of William Golding', *Kenyon Review*, XIX (Autumn, 1957), pp. 577–92.
2. Ibid., p. 577.
3. William Golding, 'Fable', in *The Hot Gates* (London, 1965), p. 85.
4. Ibid.
5. Aesop, *Fables of Aesop* (translated S. A. Handford) (London, 1966), p. 70.
6. William Golding, *Lord of the Flies* (London, 1954), p. 189.
7. Ibid., p. 108.
8. Ibid., pp. 120–21.
9. R. W. B. Lewis, *The American Adam* (Chicago, 1959), p. 99.
10. R. M. Ballantyne, *The Coral Island* (London, 1964), p. 75.
11. *Lord of the Flies*, p. 32.
12. *The Coral Island*, p. 27.
13. *Lord of the Flies*, p. 21.
14. *The Coral Island*, pp. 87–8.
15. Ibid., pp. 3–4.
16. Ibid., p. 173.
17. Ibid., p. 122.
18. *Lord of the Flies*, pp. 130–31.
19. Stephen Crane, *The Red Badge of Courage and Other Writings* (ed. Richard Chase) (Cambridge, Mass., 1960), p. 388.
20. *Lord of the Flies*, p. 31.
21. Peter Coveney, *The Image of Childhood* (London, 1967). I am indebted to this perceptive study.
22. The same kind of visual trick occurred in a 1950's film, *The Bad Seed* (from a dramatisation by Maxwell Anderson of a novel by William March), where a doll-like child actress, Patty McCormack, who looked incapable of even the most trivial breach of manners, played a vicious murderess in a plot almost wholly dependent on this visual peripeteia since the only attempt to explain her actions involved some vaguely metaphysical suggestions that some people are born with a 'bad seed' which causes them to commit dreadful acts.
23. Richard Hughes, *A High Wind in Jamaica* (London, 1965), p. 32.
24. Ibid., p. 79.
25. Ibid., pp. 110–11.
26. Ibid., p. 126.
27. Ibid., p. 192.
28. Ibid., p. 186.
29. E. L. Epstein, 'Notes on *Lord of the Flies*' (New York, 1959), p. 192.
30. *Lord of the Flies*, p. 104.

31. Ibid., pp. 222-3.
32. Ibid., p. 222.
33. Ibid., pp. 167-8.
34. Claire Rosenfield, ' "Men of a Smaller Growth": A Psychological Analysis of William Golding's *Lord of the Flies*,' *Literature and Psychology*, XI (Autumn, 1961), pp. 93-6, 99-101.
35. Ibid., p. 124.
36. *Lord of the Flies*, pp. 240-41.
37. Iona and Peter Opie, *The Lore and Language of Schoolchildren* (Oxford, 1967), pp. 141-53.
38. C. B. Cox, 'Lord of the Flies', *Critical Quarterly*, II (1960), pp. 112-17, pp. 116-17.
39. Op. cit., p. 100.
40. *Lord of the Flies*, p. 246.
41. These anecdotes are taken from an article by Robert Wallace in *Life International*, Vol. 35, No. 11, 2 December 1963, pp. 70-80.
42. Ibid., p. 80.
43. Ibid.
44. To facilitate reading, page references for *Lord of the Flies* and *The Coral Island* will be given in parenthesis after each quotation. References for both books are to the standard editions: *Lord of the Flies* (London, 1954), *The Coral Island* (London, 1964).
45. *The Hot Gates*, p. 88.
46. *The Lore and Language of Schoolchildren*, p. 172.
47. Ralph Freedman, 'The New Realism: The Fancy of William Golding', *Perspective*, X (Summer-Autumn, 1958), p. 121.
48. James Fenimore Cooper, *The Deerslayer* (New York, 1963), p. 171.
49. *The Hot Gates*, p. 89.
50. W. B. Yeats, 'Certain Noble Plays of Japan' in *Essays and Introductions* (London, 1969), p. 224.
51. *The Hot Gates*, pp. 29-30.
52. William Golding, *The Inheritors* (London, 1955), p. 42.
53. *The Hot Gates*, p. 97.
54. Mark Kinkead-Weekes and Ian Gregor, *William Golding: A Critical Study* (London, 1967), pp. 27-31.
55. *The Hot Gates*, p. 97.
56. Ibid., p. 85.
57. Ibid., p. 99.
58. *The Lore and Language of Schoolchildren*, p. 210.
59. Ernest Hemingway, *A Farewell to Arms* (London, 1966), p. 252.
60. Ernest Hemingway, 'Today is Friday' in *The Essential Hemingway* (London, 1964), p. 388.
61. Joseph Conrad, *Heart of Darkness* (Englewood Cliffs, New Jersey 1962), p. 29.
62. Ibid., p. 30.
63. *The Lore and Language of Schoolchildren*, p. 152.
64. Despite the fact that the three main characters of Ballantyne's novel

are supposed to be naïve, untutored young sailors, their conversation continually belies their supposed social standing:

'Peterkin, you're a villain. A paltry little villain,' said Jack, quietly, as he tossed the hind legs (including the tail) of a cold roast pig to his comrade; 'and I must again express my regret that unavoidable circumstances have thrust your society upon me, and that necessity has compelled me to cultivate your acquaintance. Were it not that you are incapable of walking upon the water, I would order you, sir, out of the canoe.'

'There! you've awakened Avatea with your long tongue,' retorted Peterkin, with a frown, as the girl gave vent to a deep sigh. 'No,' he continued, 'it was only a snore. Perchance she dreameth of her black Apollo. I say, Ralph, do leave just one little slice of that yam'(318).

65. James Gindin, *Postwar British Fiction* (Berkeley and Los Angeles, 1962), p. 198.

66. Ibid.

67. Ibid., p. 204.

68. Ballantyne, as one would expect, has no qualms about using the device. The three lads are locked in a hut, waiting to be executed, when they are released because a British missionary has appeared from out of the blue and suddenly converted all the cannibals.

69. *A High Wind in Jamaica*, pp. 169–70.

70. Professor Carl Niemeyer partly believes that it does: 'The timely arrival of the British Navy is less theatrical than logically necessary to make Golding's point. For civilisation defeats the beast. It shrinks back into the jungle as the boys creep out to be rescued; but the beast is real.' Carl Niemeyer, 'The Coral Island Revisited', *College English*, XII (January 1961), p. 245.

71. See bibliography.

Index

Aesop, 8, 60
allegory, 8*ff.*
apeiron, 11
Aristotle, 53
Avengers, The, 54

Bad Seed, The, 60
Ballantyne, R. M., 14*ff.*
Barrie, J. M., 19
Beelzebub, 43
Bellow, Saul, 9
bildungsroman, 53, 54
Blake, William, 18
Blyton, Enid, 25
Brecht, Bertold, 53
Brook, Peter, 24, 27
Bunyan, John, 7

Carlyle, Thomas, 12
Chateaubriand, F. R. de, 12
Coleridge, S. T., 30
Conrad, Joseph, 44, 48, 49, 61
Cooper, James Fenimore, 12, 15, 29, 61
Corelli, Marie, 19
Coveney, Peter, 19, 60
Cox, C. B., 24, 61
Crane, Stephen, 9, 17, 60

Defoe, Daniel, 8, 9, 10, 13, 14, 15
deus ex machina, 53
Dickens, Charles, 12, 18, 19, 28, 56
Donne, John, 49

Eliot, George, 8, 19
Epstein, E. L., 21, 47, 60
Euripedes, 53
Everyman, 9

fable, 7*ff.*
Freedman, Ralph, 61
Freud, Sigmund, 20

Gindin, James, 52, 53, 62
Goldthorpe, John, 12
Grande, Luke M., 54, 55
Gregor, Ian, 35, 61

Hawthorne, Nathaniel, 42
Hemingway, Ernest, 45, 61
Hot Gates, The, 7, 31, 39, 40, 41, 60, 61
Hughes, Richard, 19*ff.*

Inheritors, The, 11, 35, 61

James, Henry, 8, 19

Kearns, Francis E., 54
Kingsley, Charles, 18
Kinkead-Weekes, Mark, 35, 61

Lewis, R. W. B., 11, 60

Marlowe, Christopher, 28
Melville, Herman, 35
Miller, Arthur, 42

Niemayer, Carl, 62
non-fable, 8*ff.*

Opie, Iona and Peter, 23, 26, 43, 44, 51, 61
Orwell, George, 7, 8

Peter, John, 7, 60
Pincher Martin, 11

Ransome, Arthur, 32, 49
Rosenfield, Claire, 23, 24, 61
Rousseau, Jean-Jaques, 12, 16, 18, 54

Salinger, J. D., 13, 54, 55
Shakespeare, William, 30, 40, 50
Sillitoe, Alan, 12, 13
Spenser, Edmund, 9

Spire, The, 11
Stevenson, R. L., 32
Swift, Jonathan, 7
symbolism, 11*ff.*

Twain, Mark, 13, 25, 42

Voltaire, 7

Wallace, Robert, 61
Wells, H. G., 35
Wordsworth, William, 16, 18, 54

Yeats, W. B., 61